A handbook of

Mobile Money Business in Kenya

An inside look at the operation of mobile money businesses in Kenya

STEPHEN MUCHIRI

Copyright © 2016 Stephen Muchiri

All rights reserved.

No part of this publication may be reproduced, stored in or introduced into a retrieval system, or transmitted, in any form, or by any means (electronic, mechanical, photocopying, recording, or otherwise), without the prior written permission of the copyright owner.

ISBN: 1537748092

ISBN-13: 978-1537748092

Contents

Preface vii

List of tables ix

List of acronyms xi

1. Introduction 1
    1.1 Background 1
    1.2 What is mobile money? 2
    1.3 What is mobile commerce? 2
    1.4 M-commerce in the Kenyan context 2
    1.5 How does mobile money work? 3
2. The Economics of mobile money 14
    2.1 Payments 14
    2.2 Financial Inclusion and Financial Deepening 16
    2.3 Mobile money and financial inclusion 17
    2.4 Mobile money and financial deepening 18
    2.5 Mobile money and other financial products 20
    2.6 Mobile money and Government bonds 22
    2.7 Mobile money and betting services 22
    2.8 Mobile money and Informal financial services 23
    2.9 Mobile money and money supply in the economy 23
3. The mobile money business model 26
    3.1 Introduction 26
    3.2 Revenue model 27
    3.3 Cost Structure 33
    3.4 Profitability 37

	3.5	Value chain analysis 37
4.		Money transfer before mobile money 39
	4.1	Introduction 39
	4.2	The Money order 39
	4.3	Western Union 42
5.		Players in the Kenyan market 45
	5.1	Introduction 45
	5.2	Telecommunication companies 45
	5.3	Independent mobile money operators 50
	5.4	The Banking sector 50
6.		Under the hood 53
	6.1	The GSM network 53
	6.2	The GSM Architecture 53
	6.3	Technologies used for Mobile money in Kenya. 55
7.		Agent network 61
	7.1	Introduction 61
	7.2	How agencies work 62
	7.3	The agency business 66
	7.4	Challenges of running an agency based business 68
	7.5	Agent Configuration 70
	7.6	Agents and AML 71
8.		Accounting 72
	8.1	Introduction 72
	8.2	Transactions without overall e-value impact 72
	8.3	Transactions with possible total e-value impact 73
	8.4	Mobile banking 74

9. Risk management 77
    9.1 Introduction 77
    9.2 Risks involving the trust account 77
    9.3 Risks involving agents 81
    9.4 Risks affecting customers 82
    9.5 Compliance risks 84
10. Customer service 85
    10.1 Introduction 85
    10.2 Customer service channels 85
    10.3 Challenges in providing customer service in mobile money ... 87
11. Opinion 89
    11.1 Introduction 89
    11.2 Market share 89
    11.3 Informal nature of the Kenyan economy 96
    11.4 Social insurance and community development 97
    11.5 Mobile money is petty cash 98
    11.6 Other factors. 98
    11.7 Proposed model 98
References 102
About the author 105

Preface

Kenya has a very vibrant mobile money system. The most successful mobile money product in Kenya is M-PESA which is run by the mobile service provider Safaricom. Safaricom is listed at the Nairobi Securities Exchange so data on its performance is easily available. In its financial report for the year ended March 2016, Safaricom notes that M-PESA helped move 38% of Kenya's GDP.

World over, a lot of people equate mobile money in Kenya to M-PESA. However, there are several other operators of mobile money in Kenya. Just as in the rest of the world, these products have not been as successful as M-PESA despite the fact that millions of dollars have been invested in them. Banks have also tried to blend their business into the mobile money model with most banks having apps that allow access to their products and services directly from the phone. One of the banks has gone to the extent of obtaining a telecommunication license to be able to get SIM cards to their customers.

This document looks at the operation of the mobile money businesses in Kenya from the aspects of finance, economics, strategy, accounting and risk and there is even a chapter on the technology. As the title suggests it is not meant to be a textbook of any of the above disciplines. Each section has a very small introduction of the specific discipline. Thus for example it will define financial inclusion very briefly and quickly goes to show how mobile money has enhanced financial inclusion in Kenya.

The business model shows how the product is set up and priced. The relevant costs for each of the activities in the value chain have been given. If an entity has an approximate figure for fixed costs they should then be able to come up with the number of transactions that would be the EBTIDA breakeven point for them.

The data has deliberately been provided in Kenya Shillings. This is because there are significant variations in the dollar amounts of the figures given from time to time which doesn't necessarily relate or indicate the purchasing power or the actual value of the Kenya Shilling to the man on the streets of Nairobi. Using the dollar amounts would significantly distort the trends. However, Table 3.1 shows a trend of the average annual Kenya shilling exchange rate to the dollar from 2008 to 2016.

Due to the young age and dynamic nature of the concept, there will be products included in this document that will either be dying or will die in short while. The Yu-cash product is a case in point. Yu cash was managed by Essar Telecom. When I started working on this in 2012, the product was vigorously being marketed. Essar Telecom left the country in 2014 in an industry consolidation deal that saw Airtel acquire its customers and Safaricom its infrastructure including its spectrum for a total amount of USD 120 million. France Telkom, the owner of the Orange brand sold 70% of their stake stake in Telkom Kenya was in 2016 sold to Helios Investment Partners with a 10% going back to the Government. The Orange brand may remain for a while. It is not clear what direction the mobile money business will take after the new partners finally formalize and implement their strategy.

At the end I have a chapter on my opinion on the M-PESA enigma. There is a perception that money transfer in Kenya is the same as M-PESA. Literally millions of dollars have been invested into mobile money by other players in the telecoms market without much success. Whereas there are very many opinions on why the product is successful in Kenya, not many people have given thought to why the other players in Kenya are not doing so well

List of tables

Table 2.1 Growth of M-PESA money transfers from 2008 to 2016. 14
Table 2.2 Methods used by Kenyans to send cash home before and just after introduction of M-PESA. 15
Table 2.3 Growth in M-PESA active subscribers compared to growth in bank accounts. 18
Table 2.4 Growth in banking agent numbers compared to bank branches between 2011 and 2016. 20
Table 2.5 Comparative transaction times between mobile money, card, and cheque. 25
Table 3.1 M-PESA revenues Year on year from 2008 to 2016...............27
Table 3.2 typical customer charges for P2P transactions 28
Table 3.3 typical customer charges for withdraw transactions 29
Table 3.4 Safaricom airtime sales through M-PESA has grown from 29% in 2012 to 42.3% in 2016 33
Table 3.5 typical agent commission for deposit transactions 35
Table 3.6 typical agent commission for withdrawal transactions 35
Table 3.7 per transaction profitability analysis for different transfer bands 37
Table 3.8 customer value chain analysis for different transfer bands ...38
Table 4.1 comparing the money order process to mobile money process 41
Table 4.2 Similarities and differences between money orders and mobile money 41
Table 4.3 Major indicators for Western Union and M-PESA compared ..43
Table 5.1 One year after launch, Equitel has experienced phenomenal growth. 48
Table 7.1 weekly trend of money transfer from one of the operators in 2011. 62
Table 9.1 Daily Trust account reconciliation template...............80
Table 11.1 Percentage of adult Kenyans carrying Safaricom lines 95
Table 11.2 Average per P2P transaction value 96

List of acronyms

The telecommunication business uses a lot of acronyms. The reader may get confused and start to wonder about all these. Some are very simple, but some are technical and even the unabbreviated form even more confusing. Below is a list of acronyms used in the document in alphabetical order.

AML	Anti-money Laundering
API	Application Program Interface
ASCA	Accumulating savings and credit associations
ATM	Automatic Teller Machine
CAK	Competition Authority of Kenya
CBA	Commercial Bank of Africa
CBK	Central Bank of Kenya
CCK	Communication Commission of Kenya
EBITDA	Earnings before Interest, Taxes, Depreciation and Amortization
ETACS	Extended Total Access Communications System
ETSI	European Telecommunications Standards Institute
GDP	Gross Domestic Product
GPO	General Post Office
GSM	System for Mobile Communications, originally *Groupe Spécial Mobile*
HSM	Hardware Security Module
ID	Identification
IMSI	International Mobile Subscriber Identity
IVR	Interactive Voice Recording
KCB	Kenya Commercial Bank
KES	Kenya Shillings
KYC	Know your customer
MFI	Micro-Finance Institution
MS	Mobile Station (Mobile Handset)
MSISDN	Mobile Station International Subscriber Directory Number (Phone number)
MVNO	Mobile Virtual Network Operator

OTA	over the Air
PIN	Personal Identification Number
POS	Point of Sale
ROSCA	Rotating Savings and Credit Association
SACCO	Savings and Credit Co-operative
SIM	Subscriber Identity Module
SMS	Short message Service
SMSC	SMS Centre
SRES	Signed RESponse
SSL	Secure Sockets Layer
STK	SIM Toolkit
UGX	Uganda Shillings
USD	United States Dollar
USSD	Unstructured Supplementary Services Data
WAP	Wireless Application Protocol

1. Introduction

1.1 Background

Kenya has a very vibrant mobile money system. The most successful mobile money product in Kenya is M-PESA which is run by the mobile service provider Safaricom. Pesa means money in the Swahili language. M-PESA therefore literally means mobile money. Since its inception in 2007, M-PESA has almost been as acceptable as cash. In its financial report for the year ended March 2016, Safaricom notes that M-PESA helped move 38% of Kenya's GDP. For a service that is less than ten years old, this performance is very impressive.

World over, a lot of people equate mobile money in Kenya to M-PESA. However, there are several other operators of mobile money in Kenya. Just as in the rest of the world, these products have not been very successful despite the fact that millions of dollars have been invested into them. These are Airtel money from Airtel Networks Kenya, Orange money from Telkom Kenya (Orange) and up to 2014, Yu cash from mobile company Essar Telecom. Essar Telecom left the country in 2015. The last chapter of this book delves into why they failed where M-PESA has been very spectacularly successful.

Banks have also tried to blend their business into the mobile money model with most banks having apps that allow access to their products and services directly from the phone. One of the banks has gone to the extent of obtaining a telecommunication license to be able to get SIM cards to their customers.

Mobile money has very significantly changed financial services in the Kenyan economy. The most special thing about mobile money is the speed at which liquid value flows in an economy. While banking services typically take more than twenty four hours to send money from one individual to the other, funds sent by mobile money do not require authentication and are available for use by the recipient almost immediately the sender hits pay.

1.2 What is mobile money?

Mobile money or mobile payment system generally refers to payment services performed from or via a mobile device. More precisely, a mobile money transaction is the payment or receipt of liquid value through the mobile networks to satisfy personal or obligatory needs. Therefore,

- Mobile money transactions always involve transfer of value.
- The value is liquid i.e. it can be exchanged immediately for the same amount of cash.
- The transactions happen through a mobile network. A payment may or may not be initiated by a mobile device.
- The transaction satisfies either a personal need such as family remittance or obligatory need such as bill payment.

1.3 What is mobile commerce?

Mobile commerce (M-commerce) is the buying and selling of goods and services through wireless handheld devices such as cell phone, personal digital assistants (PDAs) or tablet computers such as the Ipad or such other tablets from other manufacturers.

Formally, "m-commerce is any transaction, involving the transfer of ownership or rights to use goods and services, which is initiated and/or completed by using mobile access to computer-mediated networks with the help of an electronic device."

1.4 M-commerce in the Kenyan context

When mobile commerce is discussed in Kenya, mobile money tends to overshadow other aspects of mobile commerce. Much more commerce is transacted in the mobile realm than these discussions gives credit for. These include the following:

- **Targeted advertisements**: For example buying of bulk SMS. These are used significantly by mobile companies but other entities can also buy bulk SMS
- **Content sales**: This is the most diverse ranging from provision of entertainment services such as ring-tones, call ring back tones, religious quotes as well as utility bill data such as water or electricity bills.

Introduction

- **Mobile banking**: This is a term used for transferring money to and from the bank using a mobile device, making payments directly to a third party using mobile devices directly from the a bank account, performing bank account balance checks and other account transactions through a mobile device or through the mobile network.
- **M-Insurance**: This is a relatively new concept where a customer enrolls and pays for an insurance policy directly from the mobile phone.
- **Micro credit**: This refers to loans applied for through the mobile phone; they are scored on mobile and paid into the mobile phone account.
- **M-invest (Planned sale of Government bonds)**: This is a revolutionary idea where individuals will buy Government of Kenya bonds by through mobile phones. The whole process, from creating the CDS account, application to purchase the bond, payment for the bond, interest and principal repayments will all happen through the phone.

1.5 How does mobile money work?

There are several underlying methods of mobile money systems in Kenya. The system described below will borrow heavily on M-PESA from mobile operator Safaricom which is the most successful as well as on Airtel money from Airtel Networks. A full discussion of the differences in the systems in use will be left for a later chapter.

1.5.1   Customer Registration

The process of becoming a mobile money user starts with registration either at an agent point or a service provider shop. This is a regulatory requirement. A mobile money operator will be going against Central Bank of Kenya (CBK) regulations if they accept to initiate a transaction with an unregistered person. To register, the following information is required:

- Full Names (as they read on the National ID card),
- Physical Address,
- Postal Address,
- Next of Kin,
- Next of kin particulars,
- Alternative mobile phone number,
- Type of identification for registration, National ID/Passport number,
- Nationality,

- Date of birth,
- Place of birth

The agent or their employee doing the registration must confirm these details against the original identification document to ensure they are accurately filled in.

At an agent point the registration details are collected through the agent phone and sent on to the mobile money system. At this point the customer has limited functionality and may only perform certain transactions. Once the details are verified, then the person can perform all available transactions.

Why is it necessary to register customers?

At this point these are not required by any regulation, best practice and the partner commercial bank will however, usually insist on them.

KYC (Know your customer) details are used for:

- Name matching against lists of known parties. Specifically important known parties may be politically exposed persons and people on the international or national list of terrorists.
- Determination of the customer's risk in terms of propensity to commit money laundering or identity theft.
- Creation of an expectation of a customer's transactional behavior.
- Monitoring of a customer's transactions against their expected behavior and recorded profile as well as that of the customer's peers.

1.5.2 Transacting on mobile money:

The SIM toolkit (STK) menu

Included in the typical customer SIM card is a small application (usually known as an applet). This application is in the form of a menu (known as STK* menu). This menu may contain several items with which the customer can interact with the telecommunications operator. These include services such as prepaid balance enquiry, prepaid credit transfer and mobile money among others. The STK menu will be used to specifically refer to the mobile money applet. Depending on the customer's choice on the mobile money menu, they may be able to perform transactions such as;

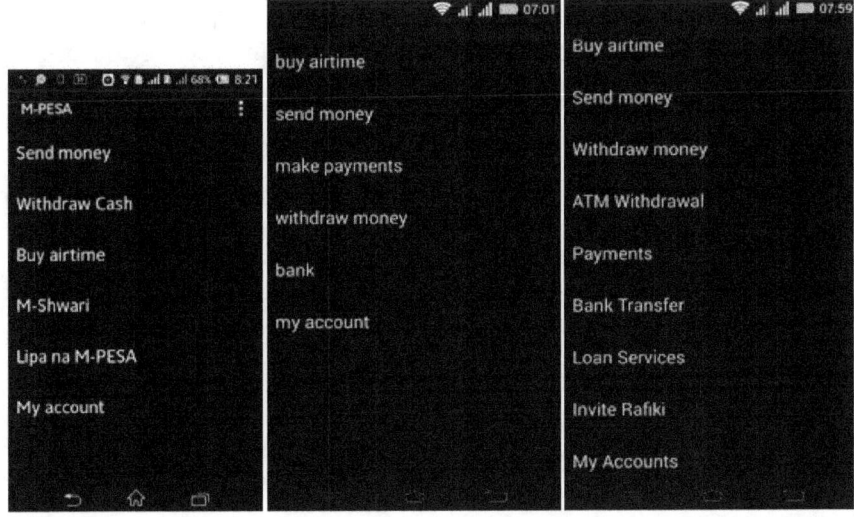

Figure 1.1 A comparative look at M-PESA, Airtel Money and Orange money Interfaces

- Send money
- Withdraw money
- Buy airtime
- Make payments
- m-banking transactions
- Other information

The picture below shows the interfaces of M-PESA, Airtel Money and Orange Money as they appear on the phone. It is worth noting the differences in the number of options available for each product. These will be alluded to in future chapters.

Deposit Transaction

When a customer walks into an agent's shop the first thing they will indicate is how much money they want to deposit. Current transaction maximums have been set at Kenya Shillings (KES) 70,000[1] per

---

[1] These balances are not relevant for real money based systems like Orange money or Equitel where the customer's account is a real bank account. The applicable restrictions on here are the restrictions based on the bank account.

transaction and Shillings 140,000 per day. However, the balance in the account should not exceed Shillings 100,000.

These maximum balances have been set with regard to global and national anti-money laundering regulations. It is instructive to note that at the point of setting up these maximums the KES 70,000 was approximately US Dollars 1,000 (2016: USD 700). Most importantly, before an operator changes their maximum balances, they have to get permission from the regulator who is in this case, the Central Bank of Kenya. These transaction maximums evolved from KES 35,000 to 70,000 in the first three years of mobile money transfer operations. This could still change as these relatively young operations grow and the customer's demands for services change.

The depositor's maximum amount may be less than the above figures if he already has money in his mobile wallet account or he is not fully approved.

The agent will require proof in the form of a National ID card or a Passport that the depositor is indeed the owner of the account.

The customer then hands in the money to the agent. The agent then confirms the amount. Depending on the risk circumstances, some agents have counterfeit detectors to confirm authenticity of the currency. The agent writes down the details of the transaction in their transaction book. These books are provided by the operator as part of agent management and take the following information for each transaction:

- Date;
- Depositor's name;
- Depositor's ID;
- Amount;
- Depositor's signature.

The agent then keys in the amount, mobile number of the customer and agent PIN. Before the transaction is processed, the agent then confirms the mobile number visually with the customer by showing them the number on the phone. Once confirmed, the agent then proceeds with the transaction.

Both the agent and the customer receive a message from the mobile money platform confirming the status of the transaction. The status may be:

- Successful;
- Delayed;
- Not successful.

A transaction may not be successful for various reasons. These include the following:

- The agent may not have enough e-value to pass to the customer.
- The customer may not be registered
- The platform may be unable to process due to technical reasons.
- The customer is trying to load more than the allowed balance;

If the message itself is delayed, the agent then calls the agent hotline to confirm with a customer service agent directly from the platform the status of the transaction.

If the message returns a successful transaction, the process of depositing cash is complete. The customer then signs the transaction book to acknowledge receipt of the value. If, however, the transaction is unsuccessful, the agent has to determine, sometimes by calling customer service the reason for rejection of the transaction. The agent is then required to remedy the situation for the customer to enable them transact.

Deposit transactions are usually free of charge to the customer.

Send money transaction

A send money transaction is referred to as a P2P (person to person) transfer. A mobile money customer may be able to send money in their mobile wallet to another customer. To initiate this transaction, a customer goes to the STK menu and selects send money. They get the option to enter the phone number they want to send to. If the sender has the number of the person they wish to send money to in their SIM contact list, then they can transfer the number from this contact list. This is important in that it ensures that the customer does not type in an incorrect phone number. So far, this process only works with SIM contact lists. The applets do not read numbers saved in the handset contact list. This number may be either a registered or an unregistered number.

The customer is then asked to key in the amount they want to send. The maximum amount a customer can send to another customer is determined by various factors.

- Whether or not the recipient customer is registered
- The balance in the sending customer's account. This has to be enough to cover both the amount to be sent and the transaction cost
- The balance in the recipient customer's account. If the intended send amount puts the recipient's account above the maximum allowed balance, then the transaction will not be successful.
- Whether or not the sending customer's account is fully approved

The customer is then asked to confirm the amount and the recipient customer.

Upon confirmation, the customer is then asked for their PIN to authenticate the transaction.

In 2015, M-PESA introduced a recipient confirmation step. Once the sender OKs the transaction, Safaricom sends an enquiry with the recipient's registered name. The sender can cancel the transaction within 20 seconds if the name in the enquiry is not the name of the intended recipient. This enquiry is based on USSD technology which we will look at in a later chapter.

If the PIN number is correctly keyed in, and the sending customer does not reject the transaction as per above, the platform is now ready to process the transaction. When the transaction is completed, a message is sent to the recipient customer alerting them that they have received funds from the sender. This message contains not just the sender number but also their registered name. Similarly, the sender gets a message confirming the details of the amount sent and the name of the receiving party. The fee for this transaction is deducted from the amount remaining in the sender's account.

The alert message to the sender may indicate success, delay or failure.

Introduction

Withdrawal Transaction

Registered Customer
Withdrawal is the conversion of value stored in a customer's account into cash. The customer notifies the agent that they intend to withdraw a certain amount from their account. The agent needs to confirm that he has adequate cash to perform the transaction. The agent requests for the customers national ID or passport to confirm their particulars.

To initiate this transaction, a customer goes to the STK menu and selects withdraw money. At this point they are asked for the agent number. Agent numbers will typically be displayed clearly and at visible place in the agent shop. They are then asked for the amount they need to withdraw. After this the customer is asked to confirm the withdrawal amount and the agent code. Once they confirm they then enter their PIN number and the transaction is processed.

The customer and the agent then get an alert confirming that the value has been transferred to the agent phone. At this point the agent can confirm that the person withdrawing the funds is the same person in the ID as the return message comes back with the customer name. The agent then enters the customer's details in their transaction book. The details in the transaction book are the same as those taken when a customer is depositing cash.

Unregistered Customer
An unregistered customer is a customer who has not undergone the registration process. For mobile money platforms that depend on a SIM based application, a customer can only register if they have a SIM from the parent network operator. For other platforms, the customer's parent network is only relevant to the extent that the mobile money platform owner may not have integrated with them. We will discuss the STK and other platforms in a future chapter. It is important to note here that a mobile number prefix is not always an indicator of the network a customer is in with the advent of mobile number portability. An unregistered recipient is a customer in any network that allows SMS and has an SMS interconnection with the mobile money operator.

An unregistered customer does not have a mobile wallet and therefore cannot get the funds credited to their account. When funds are sent to an unregistered customer, they receive a text message indicating the amount received, the senders name and a PIN to allow them to withdraw the funds. To withdraw the money, they need to go to an agent on the sender's operator to withdraw the money. If this money is not withdrawn within seven days, then the transaction automatically reverses and the funds are credited back to the sender's mobile wallet.

An unregistered customer can only be allowed to withdraw the money sent to them. They cannot perform any other transaction with these funds because they do not have an account to transact on.

For an unregistered customer, the customer presents the SMS to the agent as evidence of receipt of money. Using the PIN number, the agent transfers the value to his phone. Both the withdrawing customer and the agent receive a confirmatory message to indicate that the transaction has been successful. The agent requests for the customers national ID or passport to confirm their particulars. However unlike a registered customer, the agent is not able to confirm the identity of the person withdrawing the money from the platform.

The agent then enters the customer's details as per the ID presented in their transaction book. The details in the transaction book are the same as those for a registered customer.

Bill payment

Registered customers are able to make payments to designated merchants from their mobile wallet. The merchant may be at close proximity like a supermarket till or remote like utility companies. These transactions are referred to as Consumer to Business (C2B) transactions.

To initiate this transaction, a customer goes to the STK menu and selects the payments option. On M-PESA, this reads 'Lipa na M-PESA' which is Swahili for Pay using M-PESA. Merchants registered on paybill will have either a paybill number or nickname. The customer enters the paybill number on the next entry screen. Note that there is actually a mobile phone number underlying the paybill number. However, the mobile number is usually not publicized preferring the easier to remember paybill number. Instead of a paybill number as in M-PESA,

Airtel Money uses nick names because they are even easier to remember for the customer. To pay subscription for satellite TV service DSTV, one keys in paybill number '444900' on M-PESA. On Airtel money, one simply keys in 'DSTV'.

The customer is then asked to key in the amount they want to send.

The customer is then asked for their account number within the paybill entity. If the entity is the power utility, the customer has to key in their electricity account number to indicate who they are paying for. The use of the paybill option in mobile banking transactions will be discussed in a later chapter.

The next step is a confirmation alert. The customer is asked to confirm the amount and the paybill entity.

Once confirmed, the customer is asked for their PIN to authenticate the transaction. If the PIN number is correctly keyed in, the platform is now ready to process the transaction.

Once the transaction is completed, the paying customer gets a message confirming the details of the amount sent, the name of the receiving party and the account number credited. The fee for this transaction (where applicable) is deducted from the amount remaining in the sender's account.

Another message is sent to the merchant. If they are using a GSM POS (point of Sale) device like those used by supermarkets, the message is printed on the device. This is similar to the message printed when a card transaction is authenticated. Based on this, the merchant can then issue a receipt from their register.

For non-retail and utility companies, a dedicated link between the mobile platform and the merchant provides an update for the payment. Initially, for each merchant, a file with the records for all relevant transactions in an agreed format was sent every day at midnight from the platform. Using this file, the customer records at the merchant are updated. We will see later how the operators have provided links to merchants to make these transactions and transaction authentication real time.

Money collected on a daily basis is also transferred from the operators trust account to the dedicated Merchant bank account on demand through the operator portal or automatically on a daily basis at midnight or at such other intervals as it is collected.

Buy Airtime

To buy prepaid airtime credit using funds in their mobile money account, a customer goes to the buy airtime menu. From here they have the option of buying airtime for their own phone or for someone else. This is an especially popular mode of purchasing airtime as will be seen later on.

To buy airtime for own phone, a customer enters the amount they need to buy and then authenticates the purchase using their PIN number.

To buy airtime for someone else, a customer may enter the other person's phone number manually or as in P2P transfer, the customer could select the recipient customer's mobile number from their SIM contact list. Once the customer authenticates the transaction by keying in their mobile money PIN, the airtime credit is sent to the recipient customer and a similar amount is debited from the sending customers mobile money account.

M-banking

M-banking is the foundation of real money based systems such as Orange money. Bank based systems mean that each mobile payment account is an actual bank account with the mobile phone only serving as an access channel.

M-PESA, the dominant mobile money system in Kenya seems to have had m-banking built into it as an afterthought. It does not feature on the first level menu of M-PESA. Most of banking access for M-PESA is through USSD platforms. A customer is using USSD platform whenever they key *XXXX#. We will see in a later chapter what USSD is and how the technology works. Airtel money on the other hand has a non-bank based system that was build to accommodate access to any banks for deposits and withdrawals. 15% of the transactions on Airtel money as at December 2012 were m-banking.

Account Administration

The 'my account' menu allows the customer to interact with the operator on matters to do with their mobile money account. On this menu a customer is able to query account balance, change account PIN, and get statements and mini-statements.

Bank based mobile money systems have more options on this menu as the customer is in this case interacting with their bank rather than just their mobile money account. A customer besides the above services can access forex rates, can order cheque book or stop cheques, block their credit or debit card and more.

2. The Economics of mobile money

2.1 Payments

Research (Hassan et al, 2013) has shown that migration to efficient electronic retail payments stimulates overall economic growth, consumption and trade. In a study of macroeconomic data for 70 countries between 2011 and 2015, Moody's Analytics estimated that higher card usage contributed an additional USD 296 billion to consumption between 2011 and 2015, or a 0.1% cumulative increase in global GDP during the sample time period.

It is not clear whether a study such as Moody's Analytics has been carried out to quantify the impact of mobile money in Kenya. The table below shows the growth in value of the amounts transferred on the M-PESA platform between 2008 and 2016.

	2008	2009	2010	2011	2012	2013	2014	2015	2016
USD exchange rate (KES)	63	72	77	81	89	85	86	90	100
P2P transfers (KES Billion)	15	121	270	440	686	842	979	1,151	1,335
Other (KES Billion)	2	14	31	51	105	198	336	580	1,048
Total (KES Billion)	16		302	491	791	1,040	1,315	1,731	2,383
As % of GDP								34%	38%

Table 2.1 Growth of M-PESA money transfers from 2008 to 2016.

P2P transfers are a combination of both personal and informal business transactions. The 'other' row shows both Consumer-to-Businesses (C2B), Business-to-Consumer (B2C), Person to Government (P2G) payments for obligations. Later on we will see the reason for the jump in the 'other' transactions after 2014. There are very few Business-to-Business (B2B) transactions because by nature mobiles phones are personal.

2.1.1 Personal payments

Probably the biggest impact in the Kenyan economy from mobile payments was the enhancement of moving money from one point to the other. Cash may move for various reasons:

- Remittances to family members and friends
- Payments for personal obligations.

At the conceptual stage, M-PESA was piloted for a microfinance institution (MFI)-based loan disbursal and repayment system. This interestingly was also the first plan for the Airtel money forbearer, Sokotele. The early pilots did not integrate well with MFIs. However, what did pick up very quickly were remittances to family and friends. The table below shows the transfers in 2006 just before introduction of M-PESA and in 2008 just after the initial traction.

Period	2006	2008
	Before MPESA launch %	After MPESA launch %
Sent with family/friend	43	32
Through bus or matatu company	20	9
Post Office money order	18	0
Directly into bank account	8	7
Using money transfer services	7	0
By cheque	3	0
Paid into someone else's acount, who then passed it on	2	0
Other		5
MPESA		47
Total	100	100

Table 2.2 Methods used by Kenyans to send cash home before and just after introduction of M-PESA.

2.1.2 Utility bills and Retail payments

Utility payments are made through the payments menu in mobile money. These have steadily grown from launch of mobile money in Kenya. In its 2015 annual financials, the electricity utility company, Kenya Power, reports that 85% of their receipts come through their Easy Pay partners. These partners include; Airtel Money and M-PESA; the Postal Corporation of Kenya; Uchumi Supermarkets and banking institutions such as Post Bank, National Bank, Barclays Bank, Standard Chartered Bank, Family Bank, Cooperative Bank and Equity Bank. More than half of these are through mobile payments.

More and more utilities and other businesses such as real estate agents, are trying to get their customers to make remote payments using mobile money. Such payments:

- decongest their banking halls and offices,
- reduce the costs associated with customers facing staff and
- reduce the costs and risks of holding cash in their premises.

Retail payments on the other hand have been more sluggish with almost equal payments by card as by mobile money at supermarket checkout counters. The main reason for this is that e-payments at checkout counters do not give the same advantages as remote payments. The transaction cost for withdrawing cash at the ATM is less than the cost of making the same payment via mobile money. However, for a remote payment there is time and cost saved, explaining the preference for mobile money payment.

2.1.3 Payments for e-commerce transactions

More and more companies are accepting payments from mobile money for transactions initiated on the internet. Kenya Airways, the national carrier, accepts payments for online tickets on mobile money. Many other local companies accept mobile money payments for online purchases. Even the government accepts mobile money payments for online payments. The only way to renew a driving license from 2015 is online with the fees coming through mobile money.

This has the effect of reducing the cost for the entities receiving the payments by reducing their human resource base or as in the case of the airline, this reduces their reliance on outsourced travel agents.

2.2 Financial Inclusion and Financial Deepening

2.2.1 Financial Inclusion

Financial inclusion is universal access, at a reasonable cost, to a wide range of financial services, provided by a variety of sound and sustainable institutions. Access to financial services (financial inclusion) facilitates greater investment in productivity enhancing assets, and this increases incomes in future.

According to the United Nations, the goals of financial inclusion are:

- Access to a full range of financial services for all. These services include savings, payment and transfer services, credit and insurance;
- Sound and safe institutions governed by clear regulations and industry performance standards;
- Financial and institutional sustainability, to ensure continuity and certainty of investment;
- Competition to ensure choice and affordability for clients.

Investment is the redirection of available resources from being consumed today, to creating benefits in the future. In simple human behavior terms, people generally insist that they are unable to save liquid cash. They will prefer to have a scheme in which they do not have direct access to the money they intend to save at all. This investment may take the form of new equipment, livestock or even education for self or children.

The amount invested is expected to yield greater benefits in future than current consumption. Of course this is difficult to prove as sometimes it is difficult to measure the benefits that would accrue from an investment that did not happen.

2.2.2 Financial Deepening

Financial deepening may be defined as an increase in size and diversity of the financial system and its role and pervasiveness in the economy. To differentiate, while financial inclusion looks at the number of people that are reached by financial services, financial deepening looks at how much that populace is using the financial services.

The concept of financial deepening was pioneered by Edward Shaw in 1973. Financial deepening in an economy may be looked at as the accumulation of financial assets at a faster rate than the accumulation of other non financial assets. It may be measured as the increase in the ratio of money supply to GDP. Thus the more liquid money is available in an economy; the more opportunities exist for continued growth.

2.3 Mobile money and financial inclusion

At the launch of M-PESA in March 2007, there were only 1.5 bank branches and 1.5 ATMs to 100,000 people. However, by March 2009 M-PESA users had hit the six million mark. M-PESA was growing much faster than the bank deposit accounts in the country.

The table below shows the growth of M-PESA accounts compared to bank accounts from 2008 to 2016. Also included is the total population of Kenya during the period. To put it in perspective, 42% of Kenyans were below the age of 15 and therefore could not open bank accounts as at 1st January 2016. This would therefore seem to indicate a banking penetration of more than 100% for adult Kenyans. However, it should be remembered that a lot of people have several bank accounts.

Year	2008	2009	2010	2011	2012	2013	2014	2015	2016
Active subs (Million)	2.08	6.18	9.48	13.8	14.91	17.11	12.16	13.86	16.6
Bank Accounts (Million)	6.43	8.48	11.88	14.25	14.36	17.30	23.80	29.7	37.5
Change in bank accounts	-	2.05	3.40	2.37	0.11	2.94	6.50	5.90	7.8
Kenya Population (Million)	38.24	39.27	40.33	41.42	42.54	43.69	44.86	46.05	47.25

Table 2.3 Growth in M-PESA active subscribers compared to growth in bank accounts.

2.4 Mobile money and financial deepening

Short term savings account
Mobile money provides an account not very dissimilar to a bank account. Initially, some customers used the service as a savings account. It also allows users to convert to cash only the income they need for immediate consumption. Having this account improves the chances that money instead of being spent for immediate consumption will be held out and saved for acquisition of a productive asset. Note however that,

from a regulatory perspective the operators were not allowed to take deposits from customers.

M-shwari

In November 2012, M-PESA in a strategic partnership with Commercial Bank of Africa (CBA), launched M-shwari, a bank account operated directly from the customer's mobile phone. This account provides both a real bank deposit facility and micro loans facility to customers. The impact of the launch can be seen in the change in bank accounts in 2014 and 2015. CBA signed its 10 millionth customer on M-shwari on 06 March 2015.

CBA had always been a strong local bank and was the initial trust account holder for M-PESA. The bank is subject to Central Bank regulation and is responsible for maintaining a dedicated management information system, regulatory compliance, reporting to the credit bureau and providing capital to fund the loan portfolio. Critically, it is CBA that carries the risk and absorbs losses from non-performing loans associated with M-shwari. This ensures that the fund base for M-PESA does not change.

M-shwari is only accessible through M-PESA and is available directly on the M-PESA STK menu. Movement of funds between M-shwari and M-PESA is free. CBA matches the data collected during M-PESA registration against the Government's registration of persons database to enable remote account opening.

As at 31 March 2016, M-shwari had 3.9 million customers active within the previous 30 days. It had as at that date deposits totaling KES 8.1 billion and loans amounting to KES 7.4billion. The non-performing loans stood at 1.93% of the advances.

KCB M-PESA

KCB M-PESA is a product that is very similar to M-shwari. It was launched in March 2015 as a partnership between Kenya Commercial bank (KCB) and M-PESA. Just like M-shwari, it has registered very fast growth registering more than 730,000 accounts active in the last 30 days to the 31 March 2016 reporting date for Safaricom. It had as at that date deposits totaling KES 0.19 billion and loans amounting to KES 1.47billion. The non-performing loans stood at 3.61% of the advances.

The KCB M-PESA tries to bridge the gap between M-PESA and a real bank account in that customers can transact from the KCB M-PESA account over the counter. KCB M-PESA has also gone beyond micro loans and customers have access to loan amounts of up to KES 1 million (app USD 10,000)

Other lending entities

Due to the success of M-shwari, other smaller credit entities have moved into the mobile money credit space. These entities do not have direct contracts with M-PESA and have to do their credit scoring without the benefit of a customer's full M-PESA history. Included in these are entities like the San Francisco based start-up Branch.co, Saida and Tala. Access to their services is through mobile apps downloadable from the Google play store.

Companies in hire purchase are developing innovative technologies with mobile money. Solar power service providers such as Azuri and M-Kopa sell access to solar power on daily or weekly payments using intelligent solar home systems. Once the system is fully paid off, the customer gets to own the product for its life.

Agency Banking

In 2008, when banks noticed that M-PESA was growing beyond their wildest dreams, one of the arguments they presented to the Finance Ministry and the Central Bank of Kenya was that M-PESA was being allowed to conduct business using agents while they were not allowed to do the same.

In 2010 appropriate framework was put in place to allow banks to conduct business using agents. Commercial bank points of presence increased from 1017 branches in 2010 to 40,224 in March 2016. This resulted in a significant increase in the number of bank accounts in the economy. The table below shows the growth in bank agent points and the amounts transacted there in from 2011 to 2016.

	2010	2011	2012	2013	2014	2015	2016
Bank agents		6,513	10,066	18,082	24,645	34,381	40,224
Cumlative transactions (KES million)			13	48	93	149	171
Cumlative value (KES billion)			65	250	499	818	930
Branches	1,017	1,102	1,161	1,262	1,363	-	-

Table 2.4 Growth in banking agent numbers compared to bank branches between 2011 and 2016.

While this was strictly speaking due to use of mobile money, it was a positive disruption resulting from the introduction of mobile money.

2.5 Mobile money and other financial products

Life Insurance.
Kenya currently has very low insurance penetration rates. The rate stands at 3% of GDP compared to South Africa's 14%. Mobile insurance provides the consumer with an end to end transaction system through the use of mobile phone as customers need to register, pay and report claims via the device. It allows consumers to conveniently and cheaply take up cover as they do not need to travel to the company or to an agent to register or to make premium payments. Instead of the normal procedure of using application forms, customers require only a National ID or passport number and a mobile money account. Using the database of insured customers, the insurer is also able to send to them tailored information snippets to educate them on the value of insurance.

The first such product in Kenya is UAP's Salama Sure. With a minimum of KES 7 per day or KES 200 per month on premium, one can get a life insurance cover worth KES 100,000. With a maximum of KES 400 per month the customer will benefit from a cover of up to KES 500,000 in case of total permanent disability or death. This is affordable to most Kenyans.

Mbao pension plan.
Mbao is a corruption of the word pound. The Kenya pound, when it was in use, was equivalent to KES 20. This scheme was started for medium, small and micro enterprises to help small entrepreneurs save regularly

towards a long term and reliable income when they retire from their businesses.

Unlike UAPs Salama Sure, Mbao requires that you fill in an actual form to register for the pension scheme. Registration forms are provided by agents. The mobile number registered on the form must be the number used to make payments.

Registration costs KES 100. Insurance customers can then pay twenty shillings a day for up to a minimum of one hundred shillings a week. Upon death or retirement, the member gets back their contribution plus interest. On retirement, a member may opt to purchase an annuity instead of getting a lump sum payment. Because the scheme is registered by the Retirement Benefits Authority and Kenya Revenue Authority, customers get the same benefits that their counterparts in the mainstream pension sectors get.

2.6 Mobile money and Government bonds

In the 2015 National budget, the Kenya Government lowered the minimum amount required to purchase government bonds from KES 50,000 to KES 3000 (USD 500 to USD 30). In September 2015 M-Akiba, a platform for purchasing government debt by individuals was launched.

The first issue is expected to be a 5 year KES 5 billion government infrastructure bond with a 14% coupon rate. This bond will be purchased purely from the mobile phone. To register, a customer will use USSD code *889#. Users without Central Depository Accounts will be able to open one directly from this platform.

The minimum purchase will be KES 3000 while the maximum will be in multiples of KES 140,000 per day until the KES 5 billion is fully subscribed. Infrastructure bonds are tax free in Kenya. If this offer is successful, it will be expected to break the stranglehold that financial intermediaries and banks have had on the process of government borrowing.

Issue of shorter tenor treasury bills to the masses is expected to come on board once the government has learnt from the bond issue.

2.7 Mobile money and betting services

In the last few years, several betting companies have opened doors in Kenya. One of the big betting companies is SportPesa which in July 2016 became the first Kenyan company to sponsor an English Premier League (EPL) club. The deal saw Hull City home, away and third jersey emblazoned with SportPesa logo for three years in what Hull City said was the most lucrative deal in their 112 year history. For SportPesa, a customer is able to register directly from a mobile phone by SMS. Once the customer is registered they get their password for both mobile and web. They are also notified on the paybill number or name for their deposit. The customer sends funds to their SportPesa account using the paybill option and indicating their account number.

Once their account is funded, they are ready to place their bets. To place a bet the customer simply sends an SMS to the betting platform indicating which game they want to bet on, the team they expect to win and the bet amount. The betting platform confirms the bet with the odds and how much the gamer expects to make if he wins.

If the player wins, the funds are credited to his mobile money account unless it is above the maximum amount allowed on mobile money.

2.8 Mobile money and Informal financial services

ROSCAS (rotating savings and credit association), ASCAs (Accumulating savings and credit associations), and similar informal financial services are largely composed of people with something in common. Previously, this had been limited to people living in the same geographical regions because they have to meet regularly to bring together the cash. If one of the members of the group left the geographical region they automatically had to leave the group. However, with mobile money they can now keep their membership and continue contributing.

There are a few innovative online software for Savings and Credit Co-operatives (SACCOs) and even ASCAs that already accept payments through mobile money. This ensures that these very important financial products (Yes they may be informal but they have contributed greatly to capital formation in Kenya) continue on the same lines as the rest of the financial sectors.

2.9 Mobile money and money supply in the economy

Measures of money supply

Money supply is the total amount of monetary assets available in an economy at a specific time. Under normal circumstances, there is a relationship between money supply and prices in a given economy. There are several empirical measures of money supply ranging from M0, the narrowest, to M3 the broadest measure.

M0, the narrowest measure of money is made up of notes and coins in circulation. In a country with a significant mobile money economy, central banks must consider including the e-value in circulation as a part of this measure as it is as liquid and as acceptable as notes and coins.

Velocity of money

Velocity of money refers to how fast money passes from one holder to the other. It can refer to the income velocity or transaction velocity of money. Income velocity refers to the frequency in which the average unit of currency is used to buy domestically produced goods and services. Transaction velocity on the other hand refers to the frequency in which the unit of currency changes possessions.

The transaction velocity of money changes very significantly with adoption of mobile money. This is because mobile money transactions are easier to effect due to:

- Cheaper devices required to make the transaction compared to internet based transactions.
- Easier to make a transaction from anywhere as all that is needed is a basic 2G mobile service.
- Larger populations have access to the system so money doesn't get bottlenecked.

To illustrate,
A trader walks into his shop in the morning with no cash. He takes his car to the mechanic for service.
At 9.00 am o'clock, a customer walks into the shop and pays for his purchases on mobile money

At 11.00 am the trader sends the mechanic funds to pay for repairs on his car.

At 12.00 am the mechanic sends the funds to his spares supplier to pay for service parts.

At 2.00 pm the supplier sends the funds to his distributor to pay for bulk supplies.

At 11.59 pm the mobile money platform sweeps the funds to the distributor's bank account

Suppose these transactions were to be processed through cheque, or even as debit card processes. The table below shows the time it would take for the whole cycle to be completed depending on the medium that is used to process the payments. If the original trader did not have cash, the mechanic would have had to give him credit for his transactions or not do the work. If the mechanic could not fund the job, he would have had to take credit (probably from his bank or supplier).

Credit, either from a bank or a supplier always has a cost to it. The effect of mobile money transactions is to make available cash across different sectors and sizes of the economy very quickly reducing the cost of doing business for all by significantly reducing the need for credit. As we have seen before, where credit is needed, it is also available from formal businesses through systems such as M-shwari or KCB M-PESA. We will see later that these are just the tip of the micro credit reach available for customers in Kenya.

	Mobile money	Debit Card	Cheque
Customer walks into the shop and pays for his purchases	immediate	1 day	2 days
Trader sends the mechanic funds to pay for repairs on his car	immediate	1 day	2 days
Mechanic sends the funds to his spares supplier to pay for service parts	immediate	1 day	2 days
Supplier sends the funds to his distributor to pay for bulk supplies	immediate	1 day	2 days
Mobile money platform sweeps the funds to the distributors bank account	Same day		
Full cycle time	less than 24 hrs	4 days	8 days

Table 2.5 Comparative transaction times between mobile money, card, and cheque.

Furthermore, mobile money transactions work on weekends and public holidays compared to bank based transactions which stop working on Friday to resume on Monday. In the cycle presented above, there would be an additional two weekend days since the process spans more than one week for cheques. There is also a very big probability that the card process would also hit a weekend as the times provided are minimums and not the absolute.

Even for lay economists, even without the need for extensive research, the impact of mobile money on the GDP is clearly visible. Jobs that would not have been done at all are done. Jobs are completed quicker improving productivity. Central bank working hours, bank holidays and weekends do not have an impact on productivity as far as mobile financial services are concerned.

3. The mobile money business model

3.1 Introduction

Investopedia defines a business model as the plan implemented by a company to generate revenue and make a profit from operations. The model includes the components and functions of the business as well as the revenues it generates and the expenses it incurs. A business model is conceptual and forward thinking. It is part of a business's strategic plan at inception.

What is presented in this chapter is therefore not the business model of any of the mobile money entities in Kenya. What is presented here is what these entities do and why they have decided to do it. It would probably be a good blueprint of an entity wishing to go into the mobile money space to start from before adapting it to their unique requirements. As successful as this has proven to be, there is no guarantee that it will succeed anywhere else so it is necessary to understand it and re-tailor it to the unique customer needs of a new entity.

Components of a business model

There is no universally agreed design of a business model but most models include some or all of the components below:

- Value proposition
- Revenue model
- Cost structure
- Market opportunity
- Competitive environment

We will look at how some Kenyan mobile money companies have designed some of the above components and a bit of the why some have done it differently.

3.2 Revenue model

Revenue model describes how a business generates cash from the services it offers to its customers. It is the way a business monetizes its services. It identifies which revenue source to pursue, what value to offer, how to price the value, and who pays for the value.

The mobile money business can be very attractive in both amount and growth as shown below by the M-PESA revenues year on year from 2008 to 2016. The 2016 M-PESA revenue in the table below is in the order of several times higher than the gross revenues of competitor mobile networks in the country.

	2008	2009	2010	2011	2012	2013	2014	2015	2016
USD exchange rate (KES)	63	72	77	81	89	85	86	90	100
Revenue (KES Billion)	0.37	2.93	7.56	11.78	16.87	21.84	26.56	32.63	41.50

Table 3.1 M-PESA revenues Year on year from 2008 to 2016

The business has various chargeable activities which make up the revenue streams. Each of the revenue streams may have different ways of charging and indeed different operators in Kenya have some variations albeit few, of charging for the services. Some of the service offerings are charged internally to the telecoms business. These are detailed below;

3.2.1 Money transfer

Money transfer has three components that an operator can play with to achieve their revenue expectations depending on their customer expectations and its strength in the market. Each of the three types of transactions, deposit, withdrawal and P2P transfer may be charged or offered for free. The charges may be flat, based on value bands or may be a percentage of the value.

Deposit transaction

Deposits are typically free to the depositor. Note that deposits are the entry point into the revenue cycle and you do not want to discourage a customer from entry into the business. This also borrows from banking where cash deposit transactions are typically free.

P2P transfers

Charges for P2P transfers are based on graduated value bands. This is the real gravy train for the operator as this activity is performed directly by the customer without using resources from the operator. Other than the cost of the SMS or USSD platform which is for a mobile operator an internal resource, there is no other cost applicable to this activity.

The charge for transfers to unregistered customers, which is typically a customer on another operator's network, does involve a small interconnection fee. In the scheme of things this is minimal. However, charging for this is impacted by two factors:

- The funds are going out of the revenue generating cycle as they can only be withdrawn once they leave the registered base. The charge for this transaction should therefore take this consideration into account.

- The funds will in most cases be moving on to a customer in a competitor telecom network. The charges for this activity may therefore be built to ensure that the customer would want to persuade the recipient to move over to the sender's network.

Transaction Range (KES)		Customer Charge
10	49	1
50	100	3
101	500	11
501	1,000	15
1,001	1,500	25
1,501	2,500	40
2,501	3,500	55
3,501	5,000	60
5,001	7,500	75
7,501	10,000	85
10,001	15,000	95
15,001	20,000	100
20,001	70,000	110

Table 3.2 typical customer charges for P2P transactions

M-PESA charges are significantly higher to send cash off-net while those of the competitor operators remain the same. This is significantly due to the second point above where Safaricom would want to discourage off-net transactions and the much smaller competitors would want to encourage the same.

Withdrawal

Charges for cash withdrawals are based on graduated value bands. Withdrawal is an exit point for customer experience. If the customer can be convinced to send the e-value out to another customer instead of converting it to cash, then the operator is assured of at least one more P2P transaction charge before the funds get out of the revenue generating trip. Therefore, the operator would want the funds to remain in the mobile money ecosystem. Withdrawal fees should therefore in addition to all the other market dynamics be charged to reflect this.

Note also that the withdrawal transaction utilizes a resource as there has to be an agent present to convert e-value.

Transaction Range (KES)		Customer Charge
50	100	10
101	2,500	27
2,501	3,500	49
3,501	5,000	66
5,001	7,500	82
7,501	10,000	110
10,001	15,000	159
15,001	20,000	176
20,001	35,000	187
35,001	50,000	275
50,001	70,000	330

Table 3.3 typical customer charges for withdraw transactions

M-PESA does not charge unregistered customers for withdrawals. As discussed in P2P transfers above, this transaction is already paid for by the M-PESA customer. For the M-PESA competitors, this transaction is charged in the same way as it would be for a registered customer.

3.2.2 Bulk payments

Bulk transactions are largely B2C or G2P transactions. Bulk payment transactions may be charged to the corporate customer making the payment, or to the customer receiving the payment or to both. They may be charged on as a flat fee per transaction notwithstanding the amount, or based on a graduated scale.

Typically these transactions are charged to the corporate customer and are free to the receiving customer. The reasoning behind this is that these transactions are either payroll or very similar transactions where the entity making the payment is generally expected to take on the transaction cost.

Further, when the cash lands in the customers phone, the receiving party will either have to withdraw it, transfer it to someone else or pay a bill, all which are revenue generating. The transaction therefore needs to be more attractive to the receiving customer. Additionally, such low wage customers tend to be very sensitive to costs and through labor unions have a say in how the funds will be disbursed to them.

As these transactions are created by corporate agreements, they are usually subject of fee negotiation and the charges could vary widely. Certain customers may prefer to be charged a flat fee per transaction while others will want to be charged on graduated bands. Yet others prefer to pay on a percentage basis. Care however must be taken here to ensure that the mechanism does not get too complex for the Information Technology development as this can later on lead to other problems.

These transactions are generally repetitive and can be recurring with contracts up to three years. This provides business with assured cash flows for the period of the contract and this is also another factor to take into consideration when negotiating such charges for the transactions.

3.2.3 Bill payments

These are consumer to Business (C2B) payments. They involve moving cash from an individual account holder to a corporate utility or retail recipient. Bill payment transactions may be charged to the corporate receiving the payment, or on the customer making the payment, or to both. In the case of charitable donations the transaction may be free. All these revenue generating scenarios exist in the Kenyan market.

An operator may elect to charge both the entity making the payment and the one receiving the payment for utility bills. Airtel money charges only the corporate customer receiving the payment. A customer may determine that the overall value they get on the dominant Safaricom network on which M-PESA rides in terms of lower on-net call rates to more customers on his network is still higher than the value he would get due to the free utility bill payment proposition from Airtel money.

However, this is not cast in stone. Customers who buy lottery tickets on mobile banking have to pay for this transaction unlike the case for utility companies where the payment is made by the corporate entity. On the other hand customers making donations to Red Cross during their campaigns may make donations without a transaction cost being charged on them. No transaction costs are charged on Red Cross either as this is taken as a corporate social responsibility project.

Again as in bulk payments, bill payment agreements are largely corporate and are negotiated. An operator must therefore determine what is best for their business from an overall perspective in coming up or in agreeing the charging mode and amount to the customer.

3.2.4 Mobile banking

Mobile banking involves sending cash to or withdrawing cash from a bank. The nature of the mobile money business today is that it is still not yet powerful enough to be able to coerce banks to pay for their customer's transactions as in bill payment transactions. The result then is that mobile banking transactions are either charged to the customer or are offered free.

A phone to bank transaction is for all intents and purposes a withdrawal transaction. In deciding what to charge the customer this should be taken into account. From the banks perspective this is a deposit transaction and in the negotiation with the bank, the customer should not have to suffer additional charge from the bank as they do not charge for other modes of deposits.

Where the m-banking model is such that the transaction hits the trust account directly, the effect is that it reduces the overall e-value ecosystem and the possibilities of generating cash from that e-value in future. As such these transactions would ideally be more expensive compared to those where the banks act as mobile money agents.

A bank to phone transaction would then appear as the reverse where the transaction is a deposit transaction and ideally may be free to the customer. Where the transaction is originated through USSD, the operator's platform only serves to receive the cash and should reinforce the case for free transactions. In any case, where the operator is a telecom entity, chances are that it could be charging the bank for the USSD session. However, if the agreement with the bank is such that the bank gets paid a commission for the deposit, the mobile provider may charge the customer or institute a revenue sharing with the bank for the transaction. However, in deciding to make transactions free, it is very important to look at the price elasticity. There is no point of providing a service for free if it would not reduce the quantity of revenue generating transactions if it was charged.

3.2.5   Airtime commission

Airtime purchased directly from a mobile money account saves the telecoms business unit the cost of delivering the airtime through traditional channels. Such airtime does not involve printing, distribution and commission to airtime resellers.

This channel of selling airtime is also efficient to customers as they do not need to spend time and effort to get to an airtime reseller. A customer can recharge their airtime while sitting in the house or even when travelling in a bus just as long as they have funds in their account.

The mobile money business unit therefore gets revenue in form of commission from the telecoms business unit for distribution of airtime. Of course the operator may decide it is not necessary to report this commission both from mobile money side and telecoms side. The table below shows the percentage amount of airtime delivered by Safaricom via the mobile money channel. In 2016, Safaricom reported airtime commission of KES 9.79 billion. This approximates the cost savings from using internal channels at KES 4.1 billion which may have been reported as M-PESA revenue.

Year	2012	2013	2014	2015	2016
Airtime sales	29.0%	32.0%	34.0%	37.8%	42.3%

Table 3.4 Safaricom airtime sales through M-PESA has grown from 29% in 2012 to 42.3% in 2016

3.3 Cost Structure

Cost structure refers to the types of costs that a business incurs and their proportional split into fixed and variable costs. The concept can be applied for the smaller business units independently if the costs attributed to them can be reliably determined. The business units may be based on product, service, product line, customer, division, or geographic region.

Variable costs are those costs that are directly attributable to revenue generating activities. In mobile money these are costs such as agent commission and SMS costs. Fixed costs are those costs that cannot be directly attributed to a particular revenue generating activity. In mobile money, these include platform costs, staff costs, marketing costs, customer service costs.

A cost driven business model focus on minimizing costs for each revenue generating activity. This approach aims at creating and maintaining the leanest possible Cost Structure, using low price Value Propositions, maximum automation and extensive outsourcing. Such businesses include budget airlines, supermarkets, etc. They sacrifice quality by offering low cost.

A value driven business model is less concerned with the cost implications of a business model. These focus on value, cost notwithstanding. Such models have Premium Value Propositions and a high degree of personalized service. Luxury hotels, with their lavish facilities and exclusive services, fall into this category.

3.3.1 Variable costs

Understanding variable costs is very important in a business because variable costs determine the break-even point and ultimately the profitability of the business.

Let us break down the specific variable costs of a mobile money operation

Registration commission

Registration is the first activity that brings customers into the mobile money perimeter. In Kenya, SIM registration is a requirement of both the communications regulator and the Central bank starting from 2013. All prior registrations were done purely for mobile money purposes.

It therefore follows that ideally the cost should be allocated between the communications business and the money business based on a logical criterion. However, if the business deals purely with mobile money, then the cost is 100% applicable to the money business.

Strictly speaking, the registration costs are associated with revenues that accrue over a period of several years (matching concept). Therefore accounting for registration cost should be prorated over the average churn period of customers. This is very cumbersome to do on a customer by customer basis. Considering the value (low) and the frequency (many) of the occurrence of these costs they are generally expensed in the month they occur.

Deposit commission

Deposits convert a probable customer into a revenue generating customer. Generally as discussed in the revenue model, deposits do not attract a charge to the customer. However, once the funds are deposited into the e-value ecosystem, they cannot leave without a charge. Paying a commission for deposit is therefore sort of like making an investment for future cash inflows. Note that all P2P, C2B (Consumer to Business) or mobile banking transactions are revenue generating without an attendant cost to the operator.

Further, to be able to effect a deposit, an agent must have stock of e-value to be able to pass to a customer. This e-value represents dormant cash that has an opportunity cost to the agent. We must therefore compensate the agent for keeping the e-value stock.

Transaction Range (KES)		Deposit commission
50	2,500	8
2,501	5,000	10
5,001	10,000	15
10,001	20,000	20
20,001	35,000	40

Table 3.5 typical agent commission for deposit transactions

Withdrawal commission

Withdrawals involve the use of an agent who would need to be paid for his time and effort. To be able to effect a withdrawal an agent must have stock of cash invested. The operator must therefore compensate the agent for this investment.

Transaction Range (KES)		Withdrawal commission
50	2,500	12
2,501	5,000	25
5,001	10,000	35
10,001	20,000	60
20,001	35,000	70
35,001	70,000	200

Table 3.6 typical agent commission for withdrawal transactions

A withdrawal exits a customer from the e-value system. Such a customer will not be able to carry out a revenue generating activity until the next time they deposit cash or receive a P2P remittance. Withdrawals as noted in the revenue model attract a charge to the customer. This is the one transaction that has a revenue impact and a cost impact.

Distributor commissions

Agents may not be able to go and deposit cash with the trust account holder to get e-value. The operator may therefore wish to create super agents who collect cash from smaller agents to push e-value lower into the distribution chain.

In these circumstances then the operator would need to compensate the agent to agent transactions. Note that ordinary agent to agent transactions are not compensated since they ideally do not add value to the system.

SMS recharges

For every transaction there are usually two messages generated. For instance, a deposit transaction generates one message to the agent and one to the customer. These messages act as the acknowledgment of the transaction on both sides from the platform. From a technical perspective, the transaction itself is a message generated from the agent phone to the network. The telecommunication business where the money business is being run by a mobile operator must then recharge at a pre-agreed amount the cost of transmitting the messages.

3.3.2 Fixed Costs

At any one time the focus of a business should be to minimize fixed costs so that as much as possible the costs should be directly attributable to revenue generating activities.

The major fixed costs of a mobile money business are:

- Staff costs: These include; agent management staff, back office staff and other administration staff.
- Marketing costs: These are primarily educational and promotional costs for driving the business.
- Other General and Administration costs: These are all the other costs of the business.

As with most telecommunication businesses, the main performance indicator is EBITDA which is Earnings before Interest, Depreciation and amortization. EBITDA is arrived as by subtracting the total of fixed and variable costs from revenues.

3.4 Profitability

Based on the customer charge and agent commission per transaction band as previously discussed, we can put together a minimum profitability schedule per transaction. The profitability schedule below assumes that each amount that is deposited, will be sent in full at the same transaction band, and withdrawn in full on the same transaction band at once.

The reality is that amounts deposited are sent in several tranches, and are also withdrawn in several tranches. This implies that for one deposit amount, the operator will get several customer charges on P2P and Withdrawal. As indicated, the profitability shown in the table below is the absolute minimum per transaction.

Transaction Range (KES)		P2P Charge	Withdrawal Charge	Deposit commision	Withdraw commision	Total Revenue	Total cost	Gross Profit
101	500	11	27	8	12	38	20	18
501	1,000	15	27	8	12	42	20	22
1,001	1,500	25	27	8	12	52	20	32
1,501	2,500	40	27	8	12	67	20	47
2,501	3,500	55	49	10	25	104	35	69
3,501	5,000	60	66	10	25	126	35	91
5,001	7,500	75	82	15	35	157	50	107
7,501	10,000	85	110	15	35	195	50	145
10,001	15,000	95	159	20	60	254	80	174
15,001	20,000	100	176	20	60	276	80	196
20,001	35,000	110	187	40	70	297	110	187
35,001	50,000	110	275	50	200	385	250	135
50,001	70,000	110	330	50	200	440	250	190

Table 3.7 per transaction profitability analysis for different transfer bands

The break-even point is that volume of activity required to generate enough margins to cover the fixed costs of a business. If the total fixed costs are known, the variable costs can be graphed against the revenues to give the break-even number of transactions.

3.5 Value chain analysis

Once we have the revenues and the costs per band we can then proceed to put together a value chain analysis model. Value Chain Analysis is a useful tool for working out how we can create the greatest possible value for our customers.

From the table below it can be seen that a customer gets the best value by transferring the highest amount. We can also see based on our hypothetical data that a customer gets better value on a less than KES 100 transfer than between KES 100 and 500. Probably the operator wanted to discourage transfers of certain amounts. This may even be a fraud mitigation issue.

For a new business the operator might want to perform several scenarios of this analysis to determine at what point the customer is getting the best value vis-à-vis the profitability of each transfer band.

Transaction Range (KES)		P2P Charge	Withdrawal Charge	Minimum Transfer	Maximum Transfer	Minimum Withdraw	Maximum Withdraw	Minimum Withdraw	Maximum Withdraw
50	100	3	10	6.0%	3.0%	20.0%	10.0%	26.0%	13.0%
101	500	11	27	10.9%	2.2%	26.7%	5.4%	37.6%	7.6%
501	1,000	15	27	3.0%	1.5%	5.4%	2.7%	8.4%	4.2%
1,001	1,500	25	27	2.5%	1.7%	2.7%	1.8%	5.2%	3.5%
1,501	2,500	40	27	2.7%	1.6%	1.8%	1.1%	4.5%	2.7%
2,501	3,500	55	49	2.2%	1.6%	2.0%	1.4%	4.2%	3.0%
3,501	5,000	60	66	1.7%	1.2%	1.9%	1.3%	3.6%	2.5%
5,001	7,500	75	82	1.5%	1.0%	1.6%	1.1%	3.1%	2.1%
7,501	10,000	85	110	1.1%	0.9%	1.5%	1.1%	2.6%	2.0%
10,001	15,000	95	159	0.9%	0.6%	1.6%	1.1%	2.5%	1.7%
15,001	20,000	100	176	0.7%	0.5%	1.2%	0.9%	1.8%	1.4%
20,001	25,000	110	187	0.5%	0.4%	0.9%	0.7%	1.5%	1.2%
25,001	30,000	110	187	0.4%	0.4%	0.7%	0.6%	1.2%	1.0%
30,001	35,000	110	187	0.4%	0.3%	0.6%	0.5%	1.0%	0.8%
35,001	40,000	110	275	0.3%	0.3%	0.8%	0.7%	1.1%	1.0%
40,001	45,000	110	275	0.3%	0.2%	0.7%	0.6%	1.0%	0.9%
45,001	50,000	110	275	0.2%	0.2%	0.6%	0.6%	0.9%	0.8%
50,001	70,000	110	330	0.2%	0.2%	0.7%	0.5%	0.9%	0.6%

Table 3.8 customer value chain analysis for different transfer bands

4. Money transfer before mobile money

4.1 Introduction

The concept of money has been around for the last three thousand years or so. In the very early years, money took the form of precious metals such as gold or silver. The item itself that was money had the intrinsic value. As Central banks evolved and started issuing money, the note or coin did not carry the value, but was instead a promise to give such value to the bearer of the monetary instrument.

To buy something using money, whether in the olden days or today, the item of value has to be exchanged with, or transferred to the owner of the goods or service. Thus the concept of money transfers. Business has evolved ways of moving value without necessarily moving the item of value for ages. The bill of exchange was developed by Italian merchants to mitigate the risk of pirates in the Mediterranean sea trade routes. Thus the goods ships did not carry cash (gold) but instead a promise from the buyer to make payment.

Probably, the invention with the biggest impact was the development of accounting which allowed for the creation of trading houses and further on the banking system as we know it today.

4.2 The Money order

It feels very strange in the electronic age to associate mobile money with the money order system, especially the pre-telegraphic days when money transfer was completely manual. However, though the use of money orders and postal orders in Kenya has very significantly declined, it is interesting to note that the system is still significantly robust in western economies.

4.2.1 A history of the money order

The Money Order system was established by a private firm in Great Britain in 1792, and was expensive and not very successful. In about

1836, it was sold to another private firm which lowered the fees and significantly increased the popularity and usage of the system. The GPO noted its success and profitability, and took over the system in 1838. Fees were reduced further, and usage increased further, making the Money Order system reasonably profitable.

Regulation concerning Money Orders, which was dated 10 August 1840, Section 38

"and whereas the Postmaster General hath, with the Concurrence of the Commissioners of Her Majesty's Treasury, made Regulations by which the Public are enabled to remit small Sums of Money through the Post Office by means of Money Orders; be it enacted, That such Mode of transmitting Money through the Post Office may have Continuance so long as the Commissioners of Her Majesty's Treasury shall see fit:...."

http://www.victorianweb.org/history/letters/bootle.html 18 Dec 2011

4.2.2 How do money orders work

In Kenya, money orders are only issued by the Post office.

1. Fill and present a Money Order form and cash to the Teller / Cashier.
2. Cashier gives a receipt and an Order.
3. Deliver the order to the payee.
4. The Payee presents the order and identification document to the paying Postal outlet for cash payment.

In the background, when the post office gives you the order, they deliver the information to the postmaster in the recipient's post office. This was usually delivered by the same delivery process as with the rest of the mail. It, however, progressed to being telegraphed to the recipient's post office which meant that the recipient could ideally get the funds the same day. This was the telegraphic money order. In Kenya this fell apart with the separation of the Posts and Telecommunication entity as the telegraphic equipment used the telecoms network.

To illustrate the similarities between mobile money and money orders; Assume that Kamau goes to the Post office who are mobile money agents and sends KES 1,000 on money order and KES 1,000 on mobile money to Jane. Let us trace the journey of the two amounts from Kamau to Jane.

Money order	Mobile Money
Kamau fill and present a Money Order form indicating Jane as recipient and cash to the cashier.	Kamau presents his ID and phone number and give cash to an agent. All details go into the agent book and are sent to the platform
Cashier gives Kamau a receipt and the money Order.	Kamau receives a confirmation message. Evalue is loaded into his account.
Kamau physically delivers the paper order to Jane either directly or through the postal system.	Kamau sends the funds to Jane via the mobile platform
Jane presents the order and identification document to the paying Post office outlet for cash payment.	Jane goes to an agent and exchanges her evalue for cash and signs the agent book.

Table 4.1 comparing the money order process to mobile money process

So what are the similarities and differences between the fancy mobile money process and the archaic money order?

Similarities	Differences
Kamaus personal details in the agent book also in the money order.	Jane is not yet not known to the system when Kamau deposits the cash.
The confirmation message acts as the receipt for the cash paid in.	Confirmation of receipt by mobile money is electronic while money order is confirmed on paper
The money order in the is equivalent to evalue in your account	Money order is specifically payable to Jane for a value of KES 1,000 while the e-value in Kamaus account could be sent to any person or persons in different amounts.
The details of the funds being sent are delivered by the system which is equivalent to sending the money order by post.	Delivery of mobile money is electronic and much faster than the physical deliverly of money order.
Presentation of the order to the post office is equivalent to the recipient presenting his credentials and exchanging the evalue for cash at the agent point.	The money order can only be coverted to cash while e-value can be onsent to another customer or used to pay bills. The money order has to be presented to a specific post office while evalue can be redeemed from any agent.

Table 4.2 Similarities and differences between money orders and mobile money

A money order is an alternative to a cheque. Money orders are generally accepted (or in some cases preferred) in most situations where cheques are accepted. Sometimes a money order is the safest way to pay. It is unsafe to send cash through the mail because anybody who gets their hands on the money can spend it. However, money orders are made payable to a specific person or organization just like cheques are.

In Kenya, some schools while not accepting payments by cheque still accept money orders. Because the money order is already paid for upfront, nobody has to worry about personal cheques being dishonoured. Funds don't come from the sender's bank account - the money order is guaranteed by the Post office.

From a security perspective, when a person writes a cheque, their bank account information appears at the bottom of their cheque. If the person being paid is not known or is not trusted, one may be hesitant to hand that information over. The payee may use the information to create fake cheques, which will create headaches for the payer. Money orders allow a person to make payments without sharing sensitive information.

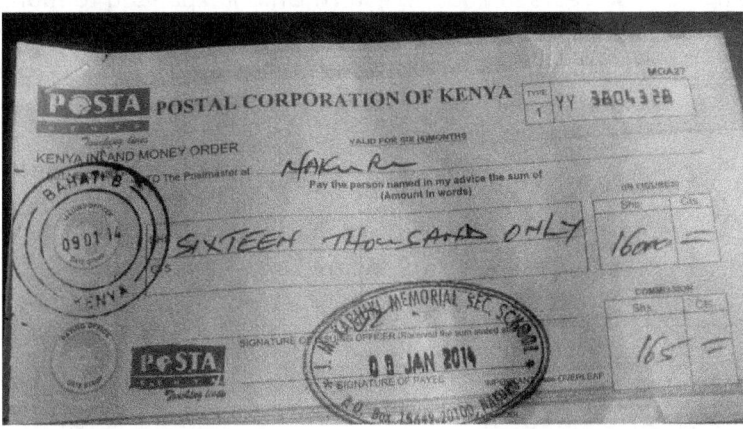

Figure 4.1 A money order issued by the Postal Corporation of Kenya

The money order shown above is a bearer instrument. It will be paid to whoever presents it to the postmaster.

4.3 Western Union

Western Union was founded in 1851 as the New York and Mississippi Valley Printing Telegraph Company. In 1856 the company changed its name to Western Union to mark the consolidation of several telegraph lines in what was then the Western-most reaches of the American telegraph system. It was one of the original 11 stocks included in the first Dow Jones Average in 1884. In 1896, Western Union provided services to Europe, Northern Africa, North and South America, Australia and Asia. In 1914, they introduced the first consumer charge card. The first commercial satellite in the U.S. was introduced by Western Union in 1974.

Emerging from its roots as a telegram business, the company evolved its services in 1871to offer electronic money transfer. However, it was only in 1980, that revenue from the money transfer service exceeded that from the telegram service. This points to the relative young importance of money transfer compared to the traditional communication needs. Today, Western Union offers money order, money transfer, payment and prepaid services. The company officially delivered their last telegram in 2006.

At the age of 150 years in 2001, Western Union expanded to more than 100,000 Agent locations worldwide. In 2016 Western Union reported more than 500,000 agent locations. We will see later on the value of agent network in a money transfer system

4.3.1 Comparing M-PESA and Western Union 2015.

In 2015, Western Union reported an average of 31 transactions per second. This approximates to just below 1 billion transactions for the year. M-PESA reported an average of 7.43 transactions per active user

	WU 2015	MPESA
Revenue (USD Billion)	5	0.4
Transactions (Million)	978	1,480
Total value transferred (USD Billion)	250	53
Countries	200	1
Currencies	130	1
Agents (Thousands)	500	100
Total available customers (million)	1,000	47

Table 4.3 Major indicators for Western Union and M-PESA compared

per month (16.6 million users). This approximates to just below 1.5 billion transactions for the year. Considering that western union serves the US and the world, and the GDPs of the Kenya stands at a paltry USD 63 billion compared to the US GDP of USD 18 trillion (2014 GDP figures from http://www.tradingeconomics.com/), it can be seen that the significance of mobile money in Kenya is tremendous. This may also point out to a very significant unfulfilled need elsewhere in the world.

The table above shows the major indicators for Western Union compared to those of M-PESA. For Western Union USD 1.44 billion of the revenue is foreign currency translation related meaning that the comparable revenues are USD 3.6 billion for Western Union vs USD 0.4 billion for M-PESA. Further the domestic transfers (US and Canada) make up only 8% of the P2P transactions making Western Union a global company operating out of the US.

5. Players in the Kenyan market

5.1 Introduction

Mobile money is largely seen in Kenya from the telecommunication angle. However, banks have been very aggressive in this space with one of the large banks acquiring a Mobile Virtual Network Operator (MVNO) license largely to drive their money transfer business. The players in this field include:

Telecoms

- M-PESA from Safaricom
- Airtel Money – Formerly ZAP, from Airtel networks
- Orange Money from Telkom Kenya (Orange)
- Equitel from Equity bank
- Yu-cash which was operated by Essar Telcom – Exited in 2014

Independent

- Tangaza Pesa from Mobile Pay Limited
- MobiCash from MobiKash Kenya

Banks.

- All banks have USSD based channels for mobile banking. Most banks have also come up with mobile banking apps.

5.2 Telecommunication companies

Airtel Money

In 2007 when Safaricom launched M-PESA, Zain, the then other mobile operator launched Sokotele, a mobile payment system in association with K-REP and Packetstream. KREP was a microfinance institution providing micro credit facilities to low income populations based on the

Grameen Bank group lending model. Packetstream was an IT innovation company.

In Sokotele cash was sent through, and picked up from a Sokotele agent. The Sokotele Agent operated a payphone unit which did both the money transfer business and operated as a public payphone. The agent had multiple business lines, selling airtime vouchers, operating a public payphone and operating as a money transfer agent.

Packetstream provided the payphone units and the technology to transfer the cash. KREP provided the first batch of customers who used the system to make deposits and repay loans through the Sokotele channel. They also provided financing to customers to acquire the Sokotele unit. In 2009 Packetstream was acquired by Safaricom largely for the stock of Wimax frequencies it had acquired. Clearly this was a very early form of mobile money. The users only got notification alerts on their phones but the transactions were not actually effected through their phones.

Soon Zain moved on to Zap. Zap was the original brand identity of the mobile money product until the company was sold to Airtel, the Indian mobile service provider when the brand changed to Airtel Money. However, the move to Zap was not without controversy. Zain felt that Central Bank of Kenya was dragging its feet on giving a go ahead for Zap, its competitive response to M-PESA. CBK finally gave the no objection to Standard Chartered Bank to operate ZAP in conjunction with Zain in 2009.

Note that the no objection for the Airtel entity is to Standard Chartered Bank, the trust account holder and not to Airtel as is the case with M-PESA where the no objection was issued to the Safaricom, the operator. As of December 2011, Airtel money held less than 1% of the market share in the money transfer market. There is no indication that this market share will grow significantly.

Orange Money

Orange Money Service is hosted on Equity Bank's mobile banking platform which gives the customers the convenience that comes with a bank account. It was launched in late 2010, long after M-PESA had gained traction in the market.

Orange money as stated is not a virtual wallet. The Orange Money account is a full bank account with full bank functionality. The back end of the Orange Money account is simply Equity Bank's mobile banking platform rebranded as Orange Money. Orange brought the channel to the partnership in the form of a STK application loaded onto the SIM.

Orange money is a mapped bank account where a normal bank account is fully integrated with a mobile channel. Therefore all money transfers are bank to bank transfers. Once again, the licensee in this case is not Telkom Kenya (Orange) but Equity bank. On this basis, the regulations applicable are those that govern the banking industry. Initially, the transfer limit was set at KES 100,000 as compared to M-PESA and Airtel moneys KES 70,000 per transaction.

Equitel

Equitel is the brand of FinServe Africa Limited, itself a subsidiary of Equity Group. Equity group is the holding entity of Equity bank, the micro finance bank better known in East Africa for its disruptive banking processes that doubled access to financial services long before the advent of mobile money.

Equity Bank already had an additive m-banking platform on USSD (*247#) known as Eazzy 247. In 2010 the bank teamed up with Safaricom's M-PESA to launch M-Kesho. With M-Kesho, Safaricom M-PESA customers could initiate opening of Equity bank accounts at both Equity and M-PESA agent shops. This product was the precursor of M-shwari which M-PESA later on launched in 2012 with Commercial Bank of Africa and KCB M-PESA which was launched in 2015. Both these products have been discussed in 2.4 (Mobile money and financial deepening). By 2012, World Bank reported that the two entities were having difficulties reaching a working agreement and the product stalled. Equity mobile banking as indicated above is also the underlying channel for Orange Money.

In 2015 Equity group launched a Mobile virtual network operator (MVNO) network on Airtel Networks Kenya Limited under a company called FinServe. Finally, Equity could give its customers access to their mobile application directly on a SIM card as the telecommunication operators did.

In order to make it convenient for customers on the other existing networks, Equitel proposed to launch on a new technology SIM card known as the thin SIM. The 0.1mm-thin SIM can be overlaid on any other standard SIM card making the phone function like a dual SIM phone. Safaricom took issue with the thin SIM technology saying that using it on top of their existing SIM could threaten the security of their SIM card. It took a year of back and forth, queries from both the Central bank and Communications Authority and even Parliament before the technology was given an OK.

Equity bank had already integrated with other mobile money operators on its existing mobile banking platform. A customer can therefore move funds from Equitel to M-PESA, to Airtel Money, Orange money or vise versa. Further Equitel to Equitel transfer limits are considerably higher than mobile money limits as these are bank based transactions.

The table below shows the growth of m-banking transactions on the equity bank platform between 2015 when Equitel was launched and 2016. It can be seen that customers have more than doubled while transactions have gone up more than three times.

	Jun-15	Jun-16	Growth
Customers on m-banking (mn)	0.89	1.99	124%
Total customers	8.27	8.97	8%
m-banking transactions (mn)	77.70	247.90	219%
Cumulative value (KES Bn)	42.30	254.90	503%
Loans disbursed (KES Bn)	2.40	23.10	863%

Table 5.1 One year after launch, Equitel has experienced phenomenal growth.

While some of the growth witnessed on this new platform was cannibalizing transactions in the existing channels, the overall effect was still much bigger growth than the bank had witnessed in the previous periods. This will be interesting to watch in the next few years. Considering the growth in customers on m-banking in the first one year is just below 20% of the banks Kenya base, the potential to keep growing at the same rate for the next few years still exists. It will get much more interesting once they start looking for customers from outside the bank.

MPESA

M-PESA is the world's largest mobile money network by number of transactions. It controls more than 99% of the telecoms based mobile money market share in Kenya. It was first conceived by Safaricom in 2005 and launched in March 2007.

The product was received very well by Kenyans and by the end of 2008; it had more than 2 million users. It had transacted more than KES 15 Billion in P2P transactions. Nothing like this had ever been seen before in the financial sector and different sectors of country were getting jittery. There was no regulation in place to manage this business. The Central bank had only issued a letter of no objection. Questions had been asked in Parliament about the possible implications of allowing unregulated money transfer services.

Banks on the other hand took issue with what they felt was Safaricom being allowed to do business without a having to go through the onerous licensing regime that banks underwent. They were doubtful whether Safaricom could meet the risk management requirements associated with a large payment system network.

Zain, the country's other mobile operator then, claimed that Safaricom was given an unfair preference by the CBK due to its large market share and Government shareholding.

The media wanted to know how Central Bank had approved M-PESA. How it was being supervised. This culminated in a public demand by the then minister for Finance for an audit into the activities of M-PESA. Central bank instituted an audit of the M-PESA system and concluded that there was no negative impact on the country's financial system by allowing M-PESA to continue operating.

In an interview with Business Daily, Michael Joseph, the pioneer managing director of Safaricom said that in March 2007 when it launched, his ambition was to recruit 350,000 customers in the first year. A month later, by the end of April 2007, the service surprised everyone, even Mr Joseph himself by garnering 52,453 customers.

Based on this, he then set a target of 1,000,000 customers for his team to be achieved by December of that year. M-PESA surprised everyone again by surpassing this target to achieve 1,300,000 customers within that period. By March 2008, at its first birthday, the service boasted 2.08 million customers. To him even the first target of 350,000 was a stretch and he did not expect his team to meet it. But it seemed like M-PESA had a mind of its own.

5.3 Independent mobile money operators

Unlike telecommunication companies, Independent operators do not have a SIM card where they can place their STK applet. They use USSD technology to help their customers access the platform. Unlike telecommunication companies, they had to start from scratch as they did not have the airtime distribution network to build agent network on top of. They also did not have the funding available from the big muscle international telecommunication companies.

Tangaza Pesa

Tangaza Pesa was launched in January 2011 as the first non-telecom mobile money transfer service. Tangaza uses revolutionary identification capability by confirming the customers fingerprint directly with the National Registration of persons database. This renders it unnecessary to carry the national ID for a transaction to be processed.

Customers use USSD technology (*321#) to access the service from any network. They are able to send funds to any network regardless of their parent network. In December 2011, the service claimed to have more than 300,000 customers and 2,500 agents.

Mobicash

Mobicash was launched in July 2011. It is not associated with a telecommunications operator. Customers use USSD technology (*365#) to access the service from any network. They are able to send funds to any network regardless of their parent network. However, they have recently introduced a web based app for Android and Windows.

5.4 The Banking sector

The banking sector was already on the mobile platform before the launch of mobile money in Kenya. However, mobile banking can be divided into two categories — additive mobile banking and transformational mobile banking. The additive model provides banking services already available to the customers through other channels on a mobile handset whereas the transformational mobile banking is largely driven by telecom companies.

When M-PESA was launched in 2007, there were already several banks offering additive m-banking services to their customers. These services included:

- Balance enquiry
- Transaction alerts
- Stop cheques
- Order cheque book
- Intra-bank transfers

What was common with all these was that they were all tied to an existing bank account. Next is a look at some of the bank driven platforms available to Kenyans directly from the mobile platforms.

Eazzy 247

Eazzy 247 is the mobile platform used by Equity bank customers. It is accessed by dialing *247#. It is also the platform as discussed used by Equitel (As indicated, Equitel is in telecoms from 2015) and Orange money.

KCB MOBI

KCB Mobi is Kenya Commercial Banks mobile platform. The web based platform is an extension of the USSD based *544# platform. It is available on Google's play store and can be downloaded free of charge. From the platform, it is possible to open a bank account and transact on it.

A registered customer can also;

- make account to account transfers,
- take a loan,
- buy airtime from all mobile network operators
- pay utility bills,

- pay school fees for selected schools,
- transfer funds into M-PESA,
- load prepaid debit card.

After the tie up with M-PESA (See KCB M-PESA 2.4 above) KCB is now more actively pushing KCB M-PESA. However, it is still instructive to note that in 2015, the 2 million customers on KCB Mobi borrowed a total of KES 2.4 billion shillings. Customers on KCB M-PESA for the same period were 4.7 million and borrowed KES 6.7 Billion.

M-Co-op Cash

Co-operative bank of Kenya started out and still is the main banker for Co-operatives. Mco-op Cash is their platform for mobile access. It is accessible on USSD by dialing *667#

Among the unique offerings of this platform are:

- A customer may be able to transfer cash from their credit card (at a fee) to their Mco-op cash account.
- Customers can make deposits and payments into Savings and Credit Co-operatives SACCO (for SACCOs that are linked)

In 2015, the service had 12.4 million transactions. Cumulatively, the bank had disbursed a total of 183,000 loans with a total of KES 4.4 Billion disbursed through the channel.

6. Under the hood

6.1 The GSM network

GSM (Global System for Mobile Communications, originally *Groupe Spécial Mobile*), is a standard set developed by the European Telecommunications Standards Institute (ETSI) to describe technologies for second generation (2G) digital cellular networks.

Phase 1 of the GSM specifications were published in 1990. The world's first GSM call was made in July 1 1991. In 1992, the first short messaging service (SMS or "text message") message was sent. The GSM Association estimates that technologies defined in the GSM standard serve 80% of the global mobile market, encompassing more than 5 billion people across more than 212 countries and territories, making GSM the most ubiquitous of the many standards for cellular networks

6.2 The GSM Architecture

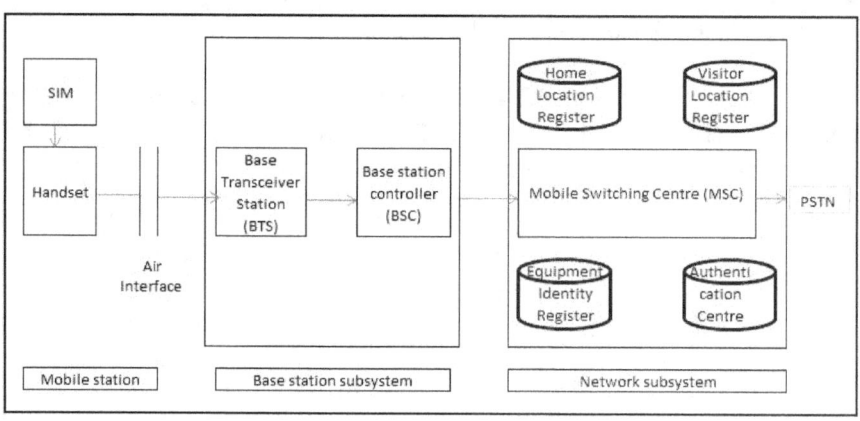

Figure 6.1 GSM architecture

6.2.1 The SIM

A key feature of a GSM terminal unit is a removable smart card module known as the Subscriber Identity module (commonly known as SIM card). A terminal unit may be a mobile phone, a Point of Sale (POS) terminal, a tablet or a net book. The SIM provides the terminal unit phone with a unique identity through the use of the International Mobile Subscriber Identity (IMSI).

The SIM is detachable and contains the user's subscription information. It may also be used to store contact data (phone book), sent and received SMS. This allows the user to retain his or her information after switching handsets. User can also change operators while retaining the handset simply by changing the SIM. Further the operator can build small applications known as STK (SIM ToolKit) applications onto the SIM. This ensures that the application is not phone dependent and is available as long as the user keeps their subscription.

6.2.2 Security Issues in GSM

The security aspects of GSM are detailed in GSM Recommendations 02.09, "Security Aspects," 02.17, "Subscriber Identity Modules," 03.20, "Security Related Network Functions," and 03.21, "Security Related Algorithms". The security mechanisms are implemented in three different system elements; the Subscriber Identity Module (SIM), the GSM handset or MS, and the GSM network.

6.2.3 Authentication

The first thing the network must do is identify and authenticate the customer. To do this the network sends a 128-bit challenge to the customer phone. The SIM in the phone then uses the A3 algorithm and the Individual Subscriber Authentication Key (Ki, Unique to every different SIM) to compute a Signed RESponse (SRES) and sends it back to the base station. If the SRES matches the pre-computed value in the base station the next step takes place.

6.2.4 Encryption and Decryption of Data

GSM makes use of a ciphering key to protect both user data and signaling on the vulnerable air interface. Once the user is authenticated, the RAND (delivered from the network) together with the K1 (from the SIM) is sent through the A8 ciphering key generating algorithm, to produce a 64 bit ciphering key (Kc). The A8 algorithm is stored on the SIM card. The Kc created by the A8 algorithm, is then used with the A5 ciphering algorithm to encipher or decipher the data in the vulnerable air interface. The A5 algorithm is implemented in the hardware of the mobile phone, as it has to encrypt and decrypt data on the fly.

The A3 and A8 algorithms are operator dependent. They are implemented on the SIM and are usually used together as one algorithm (A38) to compute SRES and Kc in parallel. These two algorithms use COMP-128 a keyed hash function. It takes the 128-bit RAND, the 128-bit Ki as inputs and outs a 128-bit value, split into: 32bits of the RAND, 32bits for the SRES, and 64bits for the Kc.

The A5 algorithm is a stream cipher. It is implemented very efficiently in hardware and the design was never made public. There are 3 different versions of A5: A5/1 a strong versions, A5/2 a weak version and A5/3 based on algorithms used n 3G phones. There is also A5/0 but it has no encryption. The reason for the different implementations is due to export restrictions of encryption technologies. A5/1 is the strongest version and is used widely in Western Europe and America, while the A5/2 is commonly used in Asia. Countries under UN sanctions and certain third world countries use the A5/0, which comes with no encryption.

There are been various cases in which cryptographers have claimed to have deciphered the A3, A8 and A5 algorithms. This would then imply that a third party can hijack a conversation or packets of data in mid air and listen in or change the data.

6.3 Technologies used for Mobile money in Kenya.

6.3.1 The SIM Toolkit based platform

SIM Application Toolkit (STK) is a technology that lets the SIM card execute a variety of additional applications. Conventionally, SIM cards are intended to store user specific data, such as phonebooks, secure user identification codes and messages, but they can also hold value added mobile applications. In 2G networks, SIM Application Toolkit (STK) was defined in GSM 11.14 standard.

The SIM Application Toolkit consists of a set of commands programmed into the SIM which define how the SIM should interact directly with the outside world and initiates commands independently of the handset.

Under the hood

This enables the SIM to build up an interactive exchange between a network application and the end user. The SIM also gives commands to the handset such as displaying menus and/or asking for user input.

It is the oldest and the most widespread application platform for mobile equipment. Due the security of SIM it is very popular for banking and privacy applications. Almost all of the GSM phones produced have been STK enabled. With developments in the mobile industry, there is less and less usage of STK compared to the on the phone applications. Around 2010, some Android models did not have STK support. This however seems to have come back as a standard in later models. Customers particularly in the developed world today have very little interaction with the STK. However the STK continues being carried as a GSM standard and even for UMTS (3G) networks.

The most popular language option used for STK development is the JavaCard variant of Java. While using Java in mobile phones has had very significant success, JavaCard/STK application development requires very good relations with smartcard producers and operators, an area where almost everything is covered by Non disclosure Agreements (NDA's). As a result it is closed community with very little if none room for independent applications.

6.3.2   The STK transaction process

a)   The applet collects transaction data. Typically the data is transmitted as an encrypted text SMS. Depending on the transaction it can look something like;
'CASH WITHDRAW 9000 **** 073XXXXXXX 999999'.

- CASH: The database table to insert into.
- WITHDRAW: Transaction type.
- 9000:   Amount.
- ****:   Customer PIN. Note that this is never stored on the database as text.
- 073XXXXXXX: Customer phone number (MSISDN)
- 999999: Transaction reference

b)   Transaction data is encrypted using a proprietary algorithm from the operator. This encryption is the biggest reason for the system sitting on the SIM card.

c) Data encrypted for SMS. This data is then encrypted at a second level. This second level encryption is the standard encryption for all SMS. This may be different for different countries or even non-existent if a country is on A0 level GSM encryption.
d) Data sent out as SMS to the SMS Centre (SMSC)
e) Data gets to the SMSC: At the SMSC, the data is decrypted for the standard encryption as in (c) above. At this point, any other SMS would have been plain text. However, the mobile money SMS still has encryption as in b above. The SMS is then sent on to the HSM for further decryption.
f) Still encrypted data sent to HSM: At the HSM the SMS is further decrypted for the proprietary encryption as in (b) above.
g) Data goes to the Platform: At the platform the data is written into the database with changes in:

- Transaction tables: These record all transactions hitting the system. This updates all relevant tables for the sender and the recipient parties.
- The balances table: This updates balances for both the sender and the receiver. As it would be very expensive to run totals every time they are requested for transactions, all cumulative totals are computed each time there is a transaction and updated in a transaction table. This is the table that is consulted each time a customer wishes to do transaction from their account. This however could be exploited as a loophole as a hacker only needs access to this one table to get cash off the system.
- Log tables: The logs tables record all non technical data to do with the transaction. These include, the incoming SMS as in (a) above, the confirmation SMS as per h below and the counterparty confirmation SMS.

h) The platform acknowledges the transactions by sending an SMS back to the initiator and an SMS to the receiving party.

As indicated the second level of encryption for the transaction is operator specific. May be one of the reasons why operators are reluctant to interconnect as it would mean sharing the encryption. However, interoperability or lack thereof has been mentioned as a most significant reason hindering the growth of mobile money systems.

6.3.3 Advantages and Disadvantages of Using STK

Advantages

- the most supported technology, highest number of devices, longest history
- low level applications, simple user interface
- SMS handling

Disadvantages
- no multimedia support (only basic pictures)
- poor independent development support

6.3.4 USSD based payment platform

When a customer dials *XXX# from a mobile phone to access a service, they are using USSD technology. USSD stands for Unstructured Supplementary Services Data. USSD is a GSM service which allows high speed interactive communication between the subscribers and applications. It is similar to SMS in the way that it allows to send and receive short text messages. It is different in the way that it is session oriented.

Since USSD is session oriented, it gives a very short delay between sending the query and receiving the response. This makes it ideal to query information from the network and to provide text content as a service. When a transaction is initiated on USSD, it holds network resources. It has to be completed fairly quickly thus USSD transactions have a tendency to time out midstream.

USSD based transactions for mobile money in Kenya are mainly mobile banking transactions. Almost all banks have basic additive applications on USSD. Bank to mobile accounts in are also significantly run on USSD.

However, many other mobile commerce uses of USSD exist. Major utilities such as power and water companies now have USSD platforms that allow their customers to interact with them. The Kenya Power app allows customers to get bills, buy prepaid tokens, make complaints, send own meter readings and many more interactions.

6.3.5 Web based mobile payment platforms

Mobile operator Yu (Essar Telcom) left Kenya in 2014. Yu cash was the only operator to feature a WAP based platform. However, the uniqueness of the mobile money entities was that they only required 2G mobile availability. As in many parts of the world, 3G availability is largely limited to urban centres. This means that a web based platform would only be available to people living in or around such urban centres with handsets that can access the internet.

A number of the m-banking platforms are slowly migrating to the smart phone interface. It is however not clear whether these apps are internet driven or are just using the smart phone interface. Certainly, there are smart phone mobile apps which initiate a USSD or SMS in the background to talk to their platforms.

6.3.6 Operator to Corporate Customer connectivity

Almost all of P2P, C2B and B2C transactions are SMS or USSD based. The unique factor of these transactions is that they all originate from a mobile device. However, linking a large utility like Kenya Power with its millions of accounts to the platform (B2B connectivity) cannot work on these retail channels.

At the beginning, as the operators learned the systems it was necessary to keep the platforms isolated from the Internet. Access was through SMS (and therefore HSM) for the individual customers. For corporate entities, this access would have to be on a leased line and static IP addresses. Eventually as the number of corporate tie-ups increased access to the internet became unavoidable. This built a case for SSL certificates. Access was now over the internet but on Https level security.

6.3.7 Encouraging innovation

Developers are coming up with products that require remote payments every day. Operators offer Paybill functionality to allow customers to make such payments. However, once these payments are done, the recipient company has to integrate them into their financial systems. This may be done in either of two ways:

- Manually reconcile the payments in the operators paybill function to their customers, a tedious and cumbersome process or,
- Build their own integration to the Paybill functionality.

To avoid this, mobile money providers have been providing APIs to customer developers to enable them access the data from the paybill directly.

In 2015 Safaricom issued an open API to developers to help them integrate seamlessly to M-PESA. These would allow the customer system to perform the following;

- Automated receipting: These extract transactions from M-PESA and credit the customer accounts in the entity's system.
- Automated payments: These allow the customer system to send out multiple payments to various M-PESA accounts. This is a bulk payment functionality.
- Automated reversals: This allows the system to reverse a transaction that has already been received by M-PESA back to the original paying customer.

7. Agent network

7.1 Introduction

The success of the postal system of money transfer largely relied on the widespread network of post offices. Long before the advent of the mobile companies and in the days of Post and telecommunication companies, every small town had a post office. Telegraphic transfers were possible because the sending post office would be able to cable the instructions to the receiver postmaster to process the money when the recipient came in.

The mobile money system takes the postal system and multiplies it a hundredfold into many small agencies spread throughout the geographical area of coverage. As of March 2016, M-PESA had about 100,744 agent points spread throughout Kenya.

The small agencies being privately owned small and micro businesses are several times more efficient than the traditional post office and banks. An average customer is able to access services more conveniently and quickly. In a significant number of the agencies, it is possible to access these services late in the evenings with services available as late as eleven o'clock in some agent points located in pubs. It is even possible to transact business on Sundays when the mainstream financial services are shut down.

Agents play a critical role in acquiring new customers, enabling them to transact and keeping them satisfied. Mobile phone companies worldwide have done a good job of developing distribution channels for airtime. In fact this is reckoned to be only bested by Coca cola. However, agent network for mobile money tends to be a little more complicated. This is due to the fact that mobile money transfers involve cash stock. This has significant security implications and successful agents are usually targets for robberies. Research indicates that up to 25% of Brazilian agents were robbed in three years after introduction of mobile money, losing on average more than USD 500 of their own money.

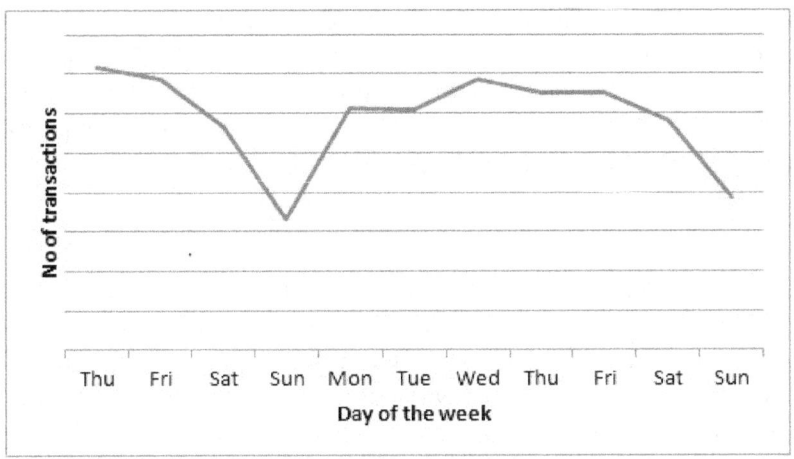

Table 7.1 weekly trend of money transfer from one of the operators in 2011.

Mobile money agents especially in rural areas sometimes have to travel long distances to get e-value stock. In comparison, airtime resellers usually get the product delivered to them and demand is fairly easy to predict.

7.2 How agencies work

7.2.1 Types of agents

The mobile money distribution channels are evolving every day. New strategies result in new and different ways of structuring the agent network. The channels described below vary from one operator to the next. Even for a particular operator they agency models keep changing as operators better understand their markets.

Direct Agents

The operator may go out and recruit their own agents and have a direct relationship with them. This ensures that the agents are answerable directly to the operator on all matters. Agents will also be more comfortable with this model since they feel that their relationships with the operator are more transparent. However, as the agent numbers grow, this could cause an agent administration nightmare. However, operators realize that what the agents are concerned most with is their revenues (agent commission). In a well developed platform, these could be done to update directly on to the agent accounts. This may be done on the fly (as and when a transaction occurs) or computed daily. This way contact between the agent and the operator could be minimized and administration made easier.

Aggregators

Aggregators are similar to super-dealers in the airtime distribution channel. They recruit their own agents and take responsibility of providing e-value stock. This model is more favorable for large well established operators who do not want to deal with thousands of small agents. The super-dealers earn a percentage of the commission for the transacting agent. However, payment of the commission is left to the operator to avoid mistreatment of transacting agents by their dealers.

E-value wholesalers:

E-value wholesalers are typically banks and financial institutions such as microfinance institutions and cooperative front office service businesses. These are businesses who handle cash in their ordinary course or business and are easily able to change large volumes of cash to e-value and vise-versa.

All commercial banks in Kenya came on board as either agents or wholesalers when they realized that mobile money was not going to go away and was going to be a significant player in the financial services sector.

7.2.2 Typical agent profile

A typical agent should preferably be an existing (profitable) business. This is because:

- The business already has its fixed costs covered by the existing business and the mobile money business only has to deal with its own variable costs. The business proposed by the operator can only increase its profitability.
- An existing business may not have to worry much about cash stock. An existing business already generates cash from its other revenue stream

and will be able to use that cash to earn extra revenue by allowing customers to use it for withdrawals.
- An existing business has already developed foot traffic and it is this traffic that will perform transactions either related to their normal purchases at the shop or for other purposes.

Where an operator opts for a new business to become an agent, the agent needs to have an extremely low cost operation with very low fixed costs. These agencies are operated from small kiosks with only the agent working from there.

7.2.3 Recruitment of agents:

A distribution employee from the operator approaches an existing business with a proposition to build another revenue stream from mobile money.

The employee asks the agent for the requirements to open an agency which are as follows:

- Duly filled in agent form.
- National ID or in the case of an incorporated entity, Certificate of incorporation and Tax PIN number.
- 2 Passport size photographs of the owner.
- Deposit slip for the first e-value amount.

Once these conditions are fulfilled, the agent is provided with an agent SIM card.

Where the recruitment is for a large network of agents as in the case of a bank, the operator might provide basic handsets for operating the agency tills as an incentive. This also separates the business handset from that of the individual increasing its availability for transactions.

7.2.4 Setting up an agents shop

First e-value stock

Once recruited, the business deposits money in trust account or with an e-value wholesaler. This deposit will be converted to e-value and sent to the agent line.

If the operator does not have a well developed chain of e-value wholesalers and the trust bank does not have a wide enough reach, the agent will need to send the banking slip to the operations back-office for the e-value to be created and loaded into his account directly. Note that this will have implications in the trust account reconciliation as it is very likely that this will not happen within the same day.

Additional e-value stock

Quite often an agent finds they have run out of e-value stock. To restock, they will need to physically take cash to an e-value wholesaler, their aggregator, or the trust account to be able to get additional e-value stock.

If however the agent can perform mobile banking from his phone, he may be able to 'pull' e-value stock from his bank account and continue dispensing it to his customers. The agent however needs to be cognizant of all the charges levied to him on an m-banking transaction and determine that for the amount he is pulling the benefits outweigh the costs.

Cash stock

An agent will need to keep a certain level of cash to ensure that customers coming to withdraw will not be disappointed. If the agent performs multiple businesses cash from other revenue stream can be used to fund withdrawals and in return earn extra revenue.

The beauty of this is that most wholesalers also take payments in e-value. The business therefore provides the double advantage of minimizing cash holding for security and earning extra revenue from this business.

7.2.5 Customer deposit process

When a customer approaches an agent for a deposit, it is typical to first ask if the agent is ready for such a deposit. This happens because the agent has to give the customer back e-value equivalent to the cash. If the agent does not have the amount requested in e-value, then the customer has to go somewhere else or take a partial amount.

If the agent is ready for the deposit;

1. Agent takes cash from the customer.
2. Request for customers ID.
3. Using the agent menu, send the e-value equivalent to the cash received.
4. Confirm the name registered on the platform corresponds to the name on the ID.
5. Write details of the transaction in the transaction book.
6. Ask customer to sign the transaction book.

7.2.6 Customer withdrawal process

Just like in the deposit process, the customer needs to confirm that the agent has enough cash to dispense. For withdrawals from large institutions such as banks, this is not an issue. In a corner shop or an agent kiosk, withdrawing the maximum amount, KES 70,000 (USD 700K as at 2016) is almost always a problem.

If the agent is ready for the withdrawal;

1. Customer sends e-value to the agent using the withdraw menu.
2. Request for customers ID.
3. The agent receives the confirmation SMS from the platform.
4. Confirms the name registered on the platform corresponds to the name on the ID.
5. Writes details of the transaction in the transaction book.
6. Asks customer to sign the transaction book.
7. Hands over cash to the customer.

7.3 The agency business

7.3.1 Revenue

Deposit commission

Customers are not charged to place money into the mobile money ecosystem. This is consistent with banking practice. However, the operator has to pay a commission for this because:

- Deposits are the starting point of the transaction cycle in mobile commerce. The operator can only run the business if there is e-value in customer phones.
- The agent is left with cash which is more risky than e-value.
- Acquisition of e-value may have a cost associate with it.

Withdrawal commission

A withdrawal commission is paid to the agent when they exchange their cash for the customer's e-value.

- This is one of the main revenue earners for the operator. It is therefore necessary to incentivize the agent to perform this transaction.
- Withdrawal is charged on the customer. This is consistent with the traditional bank charges for removing value from the system.

Recruitment commission

When an agent registers a new customer, he is working directly for the operator. Note that the new customer may never have to do a revenue earning transaction at the agent shop. It is therefore necessary to give incentive to the agent to register the customer by paying them some commission.

Other commissions:

Airtime sales
By selling operator Airtime through mobile money, agents may be compensated just like the agents who sell paper based airtime. Note that for a typical operator this reduces the printing and logistical cost involved in doing paper airtime. A customer may however be able to buy airtime directly from his phone by depositing cash into his account and buying airtime directly. However, this information is not necessarily available to customers and the agent gets a commission for evening out this information asymmetry.

Bonus commission

At the early stages of the mobile money business, the operator may decide to give incentive to agents by paying additional commissions to keep the agency business viable. These should be paid based on the individual operator's circumstances.

- They may be paid for a certain geographical region that the operator wishes to give incentive to try and grow the business.
- They may be paid for certain deposit ranges as opposed to total number of transactions. Typically, to encourage agents to keep significant amounts of float.
- They may be a simple additional percentage based on the existing commissions above.

7.3.2 Profitability:

For the system to prosper, mobile money agents have to be very widely available. Every corner shop is supposed to be a mobile money agent. Based on this thinking, the numbers of agents is very high, but the downside is that agent revenues from mobile money are significantly low.

However, as mentioned in recruitment, an operator should seek to ride on a business that is already able to cover its fixed costs base. For the agent this should be additional revenue stream meant to complement the existing business and should not add any significant costs. With this assumption, the overall mobile money revenue stream should thus be profitable even when a proportion of the fixed costs are allocated to the business unit.

Furthermore, as the business was already handling cash before, it will have built mitigations surrounding the risk of handling of cash. However, if it the business is in an area with more e-value than cash (areas with more withdrawal than deposit) this should significantly also add onto the cash handling risk mitigation.

7.4 Challenges of running an agency based business

7.4.1 Challenges of the operator

Agent recruitment

Agent recruitment can be a harrowing task especially for small operators. The agents need to be assured that for all the effort they will make, they will have a positive return on their investment. This develops into a chicken and egg situation. If there are no customers the agent business is not viable. If there are no agents, the operator cannot run the mobile money business. The operator may have to be prepared to fund some of the costs of the agent to start with if the business is going to pick up.

Access to e-value

For the customers to send money the agent needs to have e-value stock. The agents therefore need to have access to e-value before they can do business with customers. In certain cases agents have to travel long distances to access points where they can deposit cash to get e-value to trade with.

Regulatory compliance:

All the business of the operator is carried on by agents. Regulatory compliance involving customers therefore has to be carried out by agents. In Kenya it is mandatory that to withdraw or deposit cash agents have to see the customers national ID. However, if an agent turns away a customer because they do not have an ID card, this has an impact on their commission. Many agents will still go ahead and transact because they do not want to lose the commission.

Customer service:

For most customers with problems, the agent is their first point of contact with the operator. The agent must therefore be trained on the basics and have appropriate customer service skills to enable them help the customer. These skills may be hard to inculcate in the short time the distribution employee takes with an agent. However, if a customer is dissatisfied with the resolution by the agent, the customer may in their mind blame the operator even though the problem may be specific to the agent.

Fraud:

Short term looking businesses can perpetrate fraud against the customers and against the operator. The detailed frauds and their mitigations have been dealt with in the Risks chapter.

Customer Privacy:

The agent is entrusted with a lot of customer personal information especially when they do customer registration where the customer leaves personal details including copies of their national ID with the agent. This may be misused by the agent and used in fraudulent or criminal activities.

7.4.2 Challenges of the Agent

E-value asymmetry:

The main source of e-value for an agent is customers coming to withdraw. However, it is not very often that an agent finds that the deposit and withdrawal amounts are similar. There is always a difference in demand for e-value (deposits) and cash (withdrawals).

In send money home transactions, e-value moves from the more affluent cities and towns to the rural areas. Agents in cities will therefore have low e-value reserves as most of the transactions they undertake will be deposit transactions while the rural agents will be short of cash as most of their transactions are withdrawal transactions. It is not uncommon to go to small trading centres and find agents unable to perform certain levels of withdrawals particularly at the end of the month when the funds as rural folk withdraw remittances from cities. The agent will therefore be forced to either, turn away customers until they get cash or e-value or keep higher than optimal values of cash stock.

7.5 Agent Configuration

7.5.1 The agent needs a different STK menu

The functions of an agent are different from those of a customer. When an agent makes a deposit for a customer, he is moving e-value from his phone to the customer's phone. This would look similar to a customer sending funds to another customer. However, below are the differences:

- In a P2P transfer, the originating account gets a charge on it for the transaction.
- In a deposit transfer, the originating account gets a credit for the agent commission.

Should an agent mistakenly do a send money transaction instead of a deposit transaction, he will end up with a charge on his account rather than a commission. Note that this does happen in real life with agents who are not appropriately trained.

7.5.2 Agents need priority Customer service queue

Telecoms customer service centre are notorious for being unreachable. This is understandably so due to the long customer service queues resulting from to the high number of customers they serve. A lot of the problems with traditional telecommunications can find alternative solutions even if the customer is unable to reach the contact centre. However, if a deposit transaction of KES 50,000 (USD 500) does not go through for some reason, this can paralyze the operations of the agent for the rest of the day. The operator therefore has to give specific focus on agents to ensure their problems are resolved as quickly as they occur.

7.6 Agents and AML

AML stands for Anti-money Laundering. AML regulations are those regulations that have been designed to deter, detect, report and where necessary stop suspicious financial activities. Globally, The Financial Action Task Force (FATF) issues guidelines from time to time for managing the level of risks involved in the various financial services sectors.

The operator is required to observe AML regulations from time to time issued by the financial authorities responsible for AML, typically the central bank. However the transactions are performed by the operator's agents. It is therefore important that operators ensure strict compliance with AML. Thus for example, an agent should not do a transaction for a customer without proper identification.

8. Accounting

8.1 Introduction

Mobile money is a financial service. An end to end process model should among other things include the entries that need to be passed whenever a transaction occurs. This is also very important in dimensioning or evaluating the financial software that will be needed to run the business.

8.2 Transactions without overall e-value impact

Deposit Transaction

A deposit transaction transfers e-value from the agent to the customer. It does not have an overall e-value impact. However, it is also a cost to the company and crates a payable. The agent commission should be left for recording only after it has been verified.

Dr Agent   100
Cr Customer   100

Dr Agent commission   5
Cr Agent payables   5

Transfer transaction

A money transfer transaction transfers e-value from one customer to another. Where the other customer is unregistered, this e-value is held in a special account with the operator from where it the redeeming agent retrieves it.

Dr Customer1 90
Cr Customer2   90

Dr Customer1 10
Cr Revenue   10

Withdrawal transaction

A withdrawal transaction moves e-value from a customer to an agent in exchange for real cash. This transaction has a charge on the customer and a commission to the agent.

Dr Customer2   80
Cr Agent   80

Dr Customer2   10
Cr Revenue   10

Dr Agent commission   5
Cr Agent payables   5

8.3 Transactions with possible total e-value impact

Bulk payment

Bulk payment transactions usually involve a huge amount of e-value being transferred to various customers. It is rarely possible that the entity making the transfers gets the funds from an agent. Normally they have to deposit the cash into the trust account and get the e-value.

The actual bulk payments do not affect e-value because they just move the e-value from the bulk account to individual customers. What affects e-value is the process of funding the bulk account.

Bulk payment customer deposits 1000

Dr Trust account   1000
Cr Corporate customer   1000

Bulk payment customer pays 10 to an employee

Dr Corporate customer 10
Cr Customer   10

Dr Corporate customer 1
Cr Revenue   1

Bill payment transaction

Bill payment transactions are the opposite of bulk payments. A bill payment transaction transfers e-value from an ordinary mobile commerce customer to a corporate entity. The corporate entity cannot use e-value for their day to day obligations. They have to convert the amount to cash. Typically, this conversion will be set up to run after end of day processing reducing the overall e-value in the ecosystem and the trust account content by transferring actual cash to the corporate entity.

Customer pays a bill of 10

Dr Customer   10
Cr Corporate customer   10

Dr Corporate customer 1
Cr Revenue   1

System transfers 1000 cash from Trust account and destroys e-value

Dr Corporate customer 1000
Cr Trust account   1000

Deposits into the trust account

To replenish or start operating as an agent, the agent will deposit a sum of money in the trust account. This amount will be converted into e-value.

Dr Trust account   100
Cr Agent   100

8.4 Mobile banking

M-banking transactions transfer funds from a customer's mobile account to his bank account. In a simple scenario where the customer holds his account in the same bank as the Trust account, this is achieved by debiting the trust account and crediting the customer's account. Accordingly the e-value in the customer's account had to be killed to balance out the movement in the trust account.

8.4.1 STK based m-banking

Operator side

Operator to bank Customer sends (deposits) 100 from his phone to the bank

Dr Customer   100
Cr Trust account   100

Dr Customer   10
Cr Revenue   10

Bank to operator Customer withdraws 100 from his phone to the bank

Dr Trust account   100
Cr Customer   100

Note that ordinarily there will not be a charge on this transaction as it is taken as a deposit transaction.

Bank side transactions

Operator to bank Customer sends (deposits) 100 from his phone to the bank

Dr Trust account   100
Cr Customer   100

Bank to operator Customer withdraws 100 from his phone to the bank

Dr Customer   100
Cr Trust Account   100

Dr Customer   10
Cr Revenue   10

The second part is a withdrawal charge by the bank as would be charged at an ATM or even over the counter.

8.4.2 USSD based m-banking

Bank to customer

USSD transactions are typically used for bank to operator transactions. This provides a quick and non disruptive way of tying up with different banks as it does not involve a change in the STK menu every time a new bank comes on board. For these types of transactions the bank simply acts as an agent and takes cash from the customer account in exchange for e-value from its stock. The m-banking service then sends out instructions for this transaction to the mobile money platform. The transaction entries are as follows:

Dr Bank   100
Cr Customer   100

The bank will typically charge the customer for this transaction.

Paybill based Operator to Bank.

In these transactions, the customer makes a 'payment' to the banks paybill number for credit to their account number. In effect this is just a transfer of value from the customer to the bank. The customer will be charged for this transaction on the operator side as this is a withdrawal transaction.

Dr Customer   100
Cr Bank   100

Dr Customer   10
Cr Revenue   10

9. Risk management

9.1 Introduction

Risk is a fact of life in every business. It is even more so in a financial services business as and a new innovation service. While the business struggles to make sure that it is not exposed, the loophole could be looking you in the face and you don't see it for what it is until you are ripped off. As such risk can never be an exhaustive topic. Fraudsters are always watching and coming up with ways to take up what they can.

Assets may also get lost not necessarily to fraudsters but to errors, both human and system errors. Thus an innocent system patch designed to enhance the system may have very drastic loopholes built into it by error. Such updates to the system should be thoroughly documented and tested before change over.

9.2 Risks involving the trust account

Operators are expected to open a Trust account with the sponsoring bank. This trust account is held by a separate entity, a Trust which is distinct and different from the mobile operator. The funds in the trust account should be ring fenced and not available to the operator. The signatories to the trust account should be different from those of the operator. These would be appointed by the trustees.

The e-value in the whole eco system has to be supported by actual cash in the trust account.

All amounts deposited in the trust account should be converted into e-value. The process of this should ideally be automated. All funds hitting this account at the bank should have all the relevant details to convert them into e-value and transmit it through the system to the agent's device.

Employees - Operations:
Employees may have leeway to create e-value based on deposits in the bank. Despite the fact that there may be a maker-checker process,

through collusion, employees may create value into accounts in their names or in alias names.

Note that for smaller entities looking at minimizing cost, segregation of duties may not be adequate and the employees could also be able to register alias SIMs into the system. These SIMs may then be used to perpetrate fraud.

Employees: System back office:
This is by far the most dangerous risk component in a mobile money system. The IT back office employees may be able to create e-value directly into the database. Ideally this would not last very long until it is discovered. However;

Due to its young age, there are constant enhancements to the business processes that need updates to the core system. If the system can be easily manipulated by the maintenance staff, the database administrator may even be able to ensure that the fraudulent e-value is not included in the total system e-value used to do the trust account reconciliation. This may be done by simply setting an exclusion in the script that runs the e-value balance.

System maintenance team individuals can manually push funds through existing m-banking processes to their account and literally empty the trust account to their own or different accounts. Note that even with an empty trust account, the mobile money system can continue in operation until a bill payment redemption or an m-banking transaction is dishonored.

The company:
In April 2016, Central Bank of Kenya placed Chase Bank, one of the institutions under their supervision under statutory Management. This happened only after the banks statutory auditors insisted on restating the banks financial statements to include an additional KES 7.91 billion as additional insider loans.

Mobile companies in Kenya and elsewhere in the world struggle to break even. The most dangerous situation imaginable is one where the company itself decides to borrow funds from the mobile money ecosystem. They can do this by creating e-value that is not backed by cash in the trust bank account.

Unfortunately, mobile money systems are so new that it would be possible to hide these events to external auditors if the company did not borrow too much. However, as long as there is adequate real e-value out there in circulation, the operator would be able to meet their obligations using the fake e-value until the whole system collapses. Then the agents and anybody else holding e-value would not be able to convert it back to cash.

9.2.1 Mitigation

Trust bank Reconciliation

The value of e-value in the system has to be reconciled against the cash in the trust account every day and any differences between the trust account and the e-value explained . If only one activity can be done in a particular day, that activity should be the daily trust reconciliation. Although business does not shout about it, there have been cases outside Kenya where an operator woke up one morning to find no money in the trust account. While this can ideally still happen even with reconciliation, the nature of these types of fraud is that the perpetrators usually performs a test run with very small amounts up ahead and only go for the big one when they are sure their process works.

Although trust account reconciliation is reactive rather than preventative, it is the most reliable means for the operator to detect trouble in their system. Shown below is a trust account template. As expected, the reconciliation template is not cast in stone and each business may have to identify the individual items to work with. Certainly the reconciling items will be almost as variable as the businesses. Each line of reconciling items has to be thoroughly reviewed to ensure that the items included are what they purport to be and they are genuinely reconciling items. None of these reconciling items should be allowed to stay on for an unreasonably long time without being resolved.

Daily Trust Account Reconciliation	2-Jun-16
Bank Balance Movement	
OPENING BALANCE	100.00
CREDITS	20.00
DEBITS	(30.00)
CLOSING BALANCE	90.00
System Balance Movement	
OPENING BALANCE	100.00
CREDITS	20.00
DEBITS	(30.00)
CLOSING BALANCE	90.00
Variance between Bank and system	-
Variance explained by	
a	-
b	-
c	-
Total	-

Table 9.1 Daily Trust account reconciliation template

Daily balance movement analysis

To ensure no e-value is created that does not reflect on the day's balances, the day's transactions should be reconciled against the movement in the overall e-value balance. However, considering that a system may have millions of customers, this cannot be done manually. This will need to be done by accessing the system database directly.

Fortunately mobile operators already have revenue assurance teams who undertake such activities directly on huge databases and these can be used for the process. It is also important that if the scripts that run this process are to be formalized into a system, this should be separate from the mobile money system to ensure complete segregation and minimal opportunity for collusion. The team that has access to the mobile money system should also not be able to access these scripts.

9.2.2   9.2.1 Case study

MTN Uganda facing mobile money investigation (2015)
https://www.appsafrica.com/mtn-uganda-facing-mobile-money-investigation/ Retrieved 29 Jul 2016

This is one of the few mobile money risk cases that went to the media. In 2015 MTN sued six of its former employees for fraud, neglect of duty and unauthorized disclosure. The amount in the suit is Uganda Shillings 16 billion or about USD 5.3 million.

The story points to the possibility that the system or individuals either willingly or by mistake had created an additional UGX 21 million. This implies that at that point the Uganda economy had an additional USD 7 million in circulation that was not backed by cash in the banking system. Considering that this amount is just over the gross telecom revenue of some of the smaller mobile operators in a month, this can be very significant. From the operator perspective, this is also a straight forward loss unless it can be recovered from the beneficiaries, which rarely ever happens.

9.3 Risks involving agents

Registration commission
A fraudulent agent may decide to do what in the industry are referred to as kitchen activations. Here the agent takes SIM cards and registers them without selling to an actual customer for the sake of getting the commission. These may be registered to dummy customers with non-existent IDs. They may also be registered to real people multiple times.

9.3.1   Mitigation
All registrations should be checked for duplicity to avoid multiple registrations. While it is acceptable to have more than one SIM, five SIMS registered in a span of one month should be thoroughly investigated. In fact even if it was found that these accounts were transacting, these should be treated as suspicious transactions with the probability of money laundering.

Where possible the all registrations should be checked against the National registration of persons database to avoid fake registrations. This is the government database for national IDs.

Deposit commission

If the model allows for a flat commission to agents irrespective of the amounts deposited or a graduated commission where the bands are smaller at the bottom, agents have incentive to make multiple deposits for a single customer to get more commission. For large values, this tends to be quite common.

9.3.2   Mitigation

Commission data should be thoroughly scrutinized to check for multiple deposits to the same customer.

An agent deposits multiple amounts to an account and withdraws the whole amount in a single transaction. The withdrawal transaction is charged but, the total amount of commission for the multiple deposits is higher than the single charge on the withdrawal.

Check for multiple deposits to an account, which are withdrawn as a single amount without any apparent activity on the funds. They will usually be withdrawn from the same agent account or a related agent account.

9.4 Risks affecting customers

While these frauds do not have a direct impact on the company's balance sheet, they have a negative impact on the brand value of the business. Having such frauds can also reduce the propensity for customers to transact or keep value in their accounts.

Employees: Customer service

The most common fraud in mobile money is perpetrated through identity theft by or in collusion with customer service staff. In this case, a customer service agent receives a call from a customer requesting a reset of mobile money PIN. Generally, a reset changes the PIN back to to the default PIN. When a customer first accesses the mobile money menu using the default PIN, he is immediately required to change it.

Immediately the customer service agent then resets the PIN, the fraudster, either being the customer service agent or an external party who knows that the current mobile money PIN is default swaps the SIM in a short while. They have effectively stolen the identity of the customer and now have access to the funds in the customer's account. The funds in the customer SIM is sent out to another number and withdrawn in a short while. This works when there is a delay in changing the default PIN.

9.4.1 Mitigation

Customers should be sensitized to ensure that immediately they have requested for a PIN reset they should quickly change the default PIN to their own secret number.

Social Engineering

A fraudster sends a text message to a customer purporting it to come from operator. Fraudster calls the customer telling him he sent the funds to their number by mistake. Customer sends back the money without properly confirming the earlier message only to discover that the amount has been deducted from their account.

A fraudster sends a text message to a customer asking them to send the money to a particular number because their number is not working. This supposes that the customer had an arrangement with someone to send money and will only work if the customer had such an arrangement and does not confirm the authenticity of the instructions.

A fraudster purchases goods and pays by mobile money. Later on calls customer service that the funds were wrongly transferred. This is based on a lapse in customer service processes.

Agent

Customer sends instructions to withdraw funds to a particular agent. Agent insists that they have not received any instructions from the platform while in fact the funds have effectively been transferred to them.

This will only happen for a short while since when the customer calls customer service the true situation will be established. An unprofitable agent will do this and disappear.

9.5 Compliance risks

This is probably one of the least thought of but possibly one of the risks with the highest impact. Non compliance could get the business shut down by the regulator with very a significant impact on the brand perception.

With the multitude of account types being designed every day as the business grows, it is possible to have an obscure (probably no longer in use account type) programmed for a particular mobile money account. Imagine such an account with no limits on the amount held, no limits for P2P transfers, no limits to bank transfers. If such an account is then used for money laundering and or terrorist financing, this apparent slip up would completely ruin the business.

9.5.1 Mitigation

Along with the daily or periodic good practice tasks such as daily trust account reconciliation, the system has to be able to flag exceptions where unusual level of transactions happen. Editing account types or issuing of accounts other than the ordinary customer accounts should have appropriate levels of approval. When account types are no longer in use, they should be completely discontinued from the system.

10. Customer service

10.1 Introduction

Customer service is the support that a business provides to its customers before they buy, at the point of purchase and most importantly after they purchase. It is an important part of the promise the business makes to its customers. While the customers expect perfect resolutions to their problems, they do not talk about these. However, a single negative experience in this digital era can be transmitted around the world in seconds, with a significant impact on the brand value of the business.

For most people, customer service is synonymous with contact centre experience. And in more than half the cases, this is usually a negative experience. However, as stated above customer service starts even before you purchase the product or service. In this case the agent doing registration of mobile money SIM card, which may even have been telecom activation, has an impact on how the customer perceives the business.

Customer service in mobile money sits somewhere between customer service in banking and customer service in telecoms. By nature, mobile money serves the masses. Compared to banking, the charges to the customers are much less. Mobile money operators therefore cannot afford the highly personalized cost structure that banks put together. So we have a much higher population of customers to serve with much less money to do it with.

10.2 Customer service channels

There are various ways in which customers interact with the operator as part of their post sales customer journey. A customer may want to understand how to check their account balance after they have made several transactions. What happens when transactions are delayed and a customer has an angry creditor with them insisting that they did not send the funds that they were waiting for? Unlike telecommunications where a question to the operator can wait some, for money related issues, customers want responses here and now.

The operators interact with different customers for different problems differently. These include:

10.2.1 Contact centre

The contact centre is where most customers will look to when they have a significant issue to tell the operator. This will usually be a problem they need to resolve immediately or complaint about. As often happens, a customer who has sent funds to a wrong number cannot afford to wait for an hour before their issue is resolved.

It is precisely at this point in mobile money where its high speed of delivery and its liquid nature becomes the problem. A dishonest recipient of an erroneous mobile money transfer will want to quickly transfer it on to another person or withdraw the amount within a very short time. Please note that this customer could be at the other end of the country. A long queue of waiting customers in mobile money is therefore not acceptable as some may result in losses to the customer with the attendant loss in confidence with the service.

10.2.2 Self-service channels

How to questions tend to be similar and repetitive. They do not need to have to wait for an agent in a customer service queue. These may be answered using:

•   Interactive voice technology (IVR). This is useful for simple 'how to' type of questions.

•   You tube tutorials. Younger users are more likely to try and solve their own problems than wait in line if it is something they can resolve on their own. The operator should therefore incorporate some You Tube clips to explain issues that can be resolved by the customer on their own.

10.2.3 Social media

As more and more younger people start accessing services, the customer service channels will have started to move towards social media. The openness and simplicity of social media should be viewed as both an opportunity and a challenge. A customer posts something to the company's face book wall and every other customer can see that there is a problem. However, if the issue is properly resolved that can amount to a credit to the operator.

10.2.4 Agent points

As discussed previously, the agent network of mobile money acts as the face of the company. This is the point at which customers are recruited, trained and served. All these are important stages for customer service.

The operator has to make arrangements to train incoming agents and where possible keep retraining them every time there is a change in the system or in the processes or a change on the agent side. Every time there is a change in the service offerings, all agents have to be notified to avoid situations where customers approach agents for services they are not aware or familiar with. However, given the number and the reach of the agents, this can be a very daunting task.

10.2.5 Shops

Operator shops should be available to customers who are within reach to come and make enquiries and or solve problems with the service. While these are few and far between compared to agent points, there are certain things that can only get resolution at the operator shops.

10.2.6 Operator back office/technical personnel.

When all other points of contact are unable to solve issues because they are very technical and probably involve complex processes, the back office personnel should be available to resolve issues. Care must however be taken to avoid crowding the back office and issues should only get to the back office only if they cannot be resolved elsewhere.

10.3 Challenges in providing customer service in mobile money

A mobile money operator provides a service which customers expect will work. Unlike a physical product which the customer can see, consumers can't see what they are getting, until it goes wrong. This makes it difficult for companies to differentiate themselves in the market, except by focusing on price or customer experience.

As the service offering expands there are multiple services to manage and the customer facing staff are expected to know about all of them. In cases such as mobile banking, the customer is not even sure who will resolve their problems. In fact, sometimes it is only after a technical analysis of the reported issue can we tell exactly where the problem occurred and thus between the operator and the bank who should take responsibility.

M-PESA is completely dominant in Kenya. This means that the smaller operators have to manage their overhead costs on a shoestring budget, they have to keep innovating to keep the few customers they have and try to switch loyalty from M-PESA customers. They have to operate efficiently, but at the same time ensure they are delivering the right experience if they want to retain customers for the long term.

Customers want fast answers to their questions and their problems solving quickly. They want responses on their channel of choice, with many using social media to share their issues with the world on competitors to match the service they provide.

11. Opinion

11.1 Introduction

Why has M-PESA been successful while mobile money has failed to various degrees among other operators in Kenya and elsewhere in the world? The easy answer to this would be that Safaricom did something right and the others did not. It would say that by studying M-PESA, it would be possible to replicate its success.

There are thousands of opinions out there why M-PESA succeeded where others did not. Some of the factors are very superficial. Saying that Safaricom had a high market share doesn't even start to explain the situation. Further there are factors that are specific to M-PESAs parent company Safaricom and there are factors that are specific to the country.

It is necessary to look at the two sets of factors separately.

11.2 Market share

Safaricom's market share is the predominant factor that led to the growth of and, overall acceptability of M-PESA as opposed to other products on offer in the country. Normally for such a service to be acceptable to everyone, it would need to be acceptable across all the telecom networks. This is known as interoperability. However, due to this high market share the need for interoperability became almost unnecessary. This in turn led to even further growth of Safaricom's market share in the country.

We will show later that in 2016 more than 90% of economically active Kenyans have a Safaricom line and can therefore transact on M-PESA.

11.2.1 Very powerful brand identity

Safaricom has a very powerful brand. The brand equity has grown from 85% in 2014 to 89% in 2016. No doubt a lot of resources have been invested to create the brand. Products like M-PESA have delivered value to their customers. Their data network is the most widespread in the country. Even more it is a listed company with hundreds of thousands of small shareholders.

In 2014, the company spent KES 8.05 billion down from KES 9.7 billion in 2013 in print and electronic media advertisements. This is almost 10% of the KES 85 billion spent in 2014 in the two media channels.

11.2.2 Regulatory free hand

We have already seen how in 2007 the Central Bank of Kenya allowed Safaricom to launch the M-PESA business with no regulatory framework in place. This has been hailed as the bold move that allowed mobile money to make its mark in the world. The risks associated with this are best seen in the MTN Uganda case which is discussed in the Risk chapter. Had a similar thing happened in Kenya either with Safaricom or with one of the other smaller operators, the regulator would have been hard pressed to explain how such a service was allowed to launch without an appropriate regulatory framework in place. Further, the cases below show that this was not an isolated incident.

Mobile telecommunications were introduced in Kenya in 1997 by the then incumbent telecoms provider Kenya Posts and Telecommunication Corporation. In 1999 going by the global trends KPTC was split into three entities,

- Telkom Kenya, the telecommunications services provider.
- Postal Corporation of Kenya, the Postal services provider.
- Communications Commission of Kenya, the regulator.

At this time Safaricom was a business unit of Telkom Kenya at this time. In May 2000, Safaricom became an autonomous entity. The entity was a joint venture between Telkom Kenya, the still government owned fixed line provider holding 60% of the shares and Vodafone of United Kingdom holding 40%.

From the launch of Safaricom, despite having majority government ownership, the new company operated as a private entity with none of the restrictions accorded to publicly owned businesses. The regulations applicable to its parent company Telkom Kenya did not apply to Safaricom. It is not clear how the government exempted Safaricom from these regulations. This was not necessarily a bad thing for the company and for the economy as long as things went on right.

However, on 17 May 2016, the Daily Nation reported that a value for money audit by KPMG covering the period September 2013 and August 2015 implicated top managers in an alleged multi-billion shilling tendering irregularities. At this time however, Safaricom was no longer considered a public sector company since government shareholding was below 50%. Public sector company audits include a value for money aspect. This is taken up by the Parliamentary investments committee and thoroughly scrutinized. We will never be able to tell whether this would have unearthed something similar had it happened in 2003 and not 2016. Maybe the returns Safaricom was declaring to its shareholders would have been higher than were actually reported. What if rather than being the most profitable company in the region Safaricom had lost money?

In 2000 when the mobile companies started operations in Kenya the mobile interconnect rates were set at KES 16 per minute. Mobile interconnection or termination rate is the amount paid by the company that originates a call (and hence bills the customer) to the network terminating the call. This was always supposed to be at the actual cost of terminating the call. This meant that calls from one mobile network to the other (off-net calls) had to compensate the originating network for this cost and make some revenue. The average cost per minute for mobile calls on the same network (on-net) was about KES 25. Calls to other networks therefore had to cost about KES 16 plus KES 25 or KES 41 to make sense. Even as late as 2006 some tariffs had off-net calls at KES 50. It was too expensive for customers to make off-net calls. It wasn't difficult to see that whoever won this fight won the country. Mobile telecommunication was set to be a monopoly business.

By 2002, the Kenyan customers had started to coalesce into a club around Safaricom whose calls were billed per second compared to Kencell who were billing per minute. In 2006 the communications regulator commissioned Analysis Mason, an international authority on interconnection to conduct a study on the costs for terminating calls. The commission then made a determination in which the rate was dropped to KES 6.28. In 2010, Analysis Mason conducted another study in which they determined that the actual cost of terminating an off-net call was KES 0.86. It would have been very interesting to know what the actual cost for this was in 2001 considering the 16 shillings for mobile termination and KES 23 for fixed termination. It is possible that all along consumers were being grossly overcharged for off-net calls. It is also possible that Kenya would not have developed into a monopoly telecoms country if the communications regulator had properly analyzed and regulated interconnection rates from the start.

In March 2010, Safaricom reported 78.3% customer market share and 84.3% revenue market share. In the same year, the then communications regulator issued a new set of dominance regulation. Safaricom threatened the regulator with legal action. The then information minister hired a United Kingdom consultancy firm Frontier Economics to review the new competition rules. This changed the dominance threshold from 25% to 40 – 50%. Despite the fact that the Safaricom market share continued to climb, the telecoms provider was never declared dominant.

Instead, in December 2015, parliament passed the miscellaneous amendment bill 2015. Based on this, the communications regulator will have to consult the Competition Authority of Kenya (CAK) before making a declaration of dominance and when assessing critical industry factors such as Significant Market Power.

From the onset, Safaricom included onerous exclusivity clauses in its M-PESA agent agreements. This meant that if you were an M-PESA agent you were barred from doing business with any other mobile money operator. You were also barred from doing business as an agent for a bank. In 2012, Airtel Networks Kenya filed a petition with the Competition Authority of Kenya (CAK) asking the regulator to compel Safaricom to open up its agent network. Two years later, in July 2014, with M-PESA already at 18 million registered users, Safaricom agreed to allow its agents to transact business with rival entities. More than two months later, on 03 October 2014, the Competition Authority published an order directing Safaricom to allow agents to do business with competing entities. It should be remembered that by this time, the more powerful banks had entered the fray with agency banking. Chances are that without pressure from the banking fraternity, this would never have happened.

11.2.3 Weak competition

KenCell brand instability

In October 2000, KenCell, a second GSM mobile operator launched in the country. It was jointly owned by Vivendi of France (60%) and Sameer Group, (40%). In March 2004, Sameer Group exercising its pre-emptive rights on the 60% shareholding bought the Vivendi shares and sold them to Celtel Group within an hour. The company was promptly rebranded Celtel.

In April 2005, Celtel International, the parent company of Celtel Kenya was sold to Zain. In 2008 the individual Celtel companies were rebranded to Zain. Note that Zain was just a brand and did not change the company name. The brand change came almost three years after the global acquisition of the company.

In 2010, the Zain sold its sub Saharan entities to Airtel of India. This was followed by a rebrand in November 2010. To date, there are Kenyans who still refer to the company by its former name Zain. The mobile money brand Zap which had been used from 2008 was changed to Airtel Money.

All these rebrands sent mixed signals to the market and left the second mobile entity limping. It was a brand that Kenyans could not identify because it kept shifting. It was going to be very difficult to trust them with money.

Yu was doomed from the start

In 2003, a third mobile provider was licensed. However, it took five years, to start operations. In 2008, Essar Telecom launched Yu, the third mobile provider. Econet Wireless, the original licensee had been through court battles for and the local shareholders changed at least once.

Despite being heralded as the third mobile operator, Essar Telecom actually lauched after Orange, the fourth mobile operator. It did not stand a chance. In a few years, Essar Telecom was in the market looking for an investor to take up its Kenyan subsidiary which was stunted. It was not going to be easy to get a buyer for the company in a market which was dominated by a single player. Ultimately the company was sold piecemeal to Safaricom who bought the infrastructure (including the spectrum) and Airtel who bought the customer base and continue to run the Yu brand for a sum of USD 120 million.

What is however interesting in this company was that Essar of India, the parent company of Essar Telecom Kenya Limited had a very clear relationship with Vodafone, the parent company of Safaricom. Was Vodafone coming into Kenya through Essar to compete with one of its most profitable associates Safaricom? Was Essar Telecom ever meant to succeed in Kenya or was it a decoy meant to confuse the rest of the market?

Orange was not ready for the competition in Kenya.

In 2007, after extensive deliberations, the government of Kenya finally managed to get Vodafone to agree to remove its non-competition clause from the agreement with Telkom Kenya, the other shareholder of Safaricom. The ownership of Safaricom was transferred from Telkom Kenya directly to Treasury.

Telkom could now operate its own mobile network. After due diligence, various companies bid for 51% shareholding in the restructured entity. This was won by France Telkom for USD 390 million. Telkom Kenya, rebranded to Orange. However, as with the other telecoms in the country, Orange failed to generate profits. Over, the company needed shareholder cash injection. The government found it difficult to inject in more cash. It was therefore forced to cede shareholding to France Telkom for various additional cash injections. The shareholding ended up at 70/30 for France Telecom and Government of Kenya.

In November 2015, Helios Investment partners announced their intention to purchase the entire stake of France Telecom in Telkom Kenya. The government negotiated its shareholding back to 40%. This was finally given regulatory approval in June 2016. It is not clear what brand the new entity will use yet.

11.2.4 Safaricom's Actual Market Share

In the March 2016 Financial results, Safaricom reports a market share of 64.7%. To come up with the market share, each operator reports its customers to the regulator. However, there are no clear guidelines as to who is a customer. There are several ways in which telecommunication companies report customer numbers;

- Total base: All SIM cards activated.
- 90 days base: All customers who have been active in the last 90 days.
- 30 days base: All customers active in the last 30 days.

However, even when operators report based on customer activity, this is also not clearly defined. There are also various definitions of customer activity. These range from customers who have originated calls, customers who have received or originated calls, customers who have made chargeable events etc. Even if the communication authority made a clear definition, it allows operators to freely self declare and cannot possibly police the numbers.

As a result of the dominance rules, Safaricom would prefer to report as low market share as possible to keep public perception that they are not dominant. On the other hand for purposes of reporting and valuation of their companies, the management of the competitor networks would prefer to show higher market shares. All the players in the market are therefore accommodated. In reality each uses a different definition of customer numbers. The reported customer market share may therefore not mean much if the specification upon which it is built is not clearly defined.

Safaricom market share

Kenya is what is described as a multi-SIM country. Most people who have connectivity to the smaller networks also have a Safaricom line. This line may be a SIM in a dual SIM phone or in the pocket.

To come up with the real market share for Safaricom, assume that kids are only allowed mobile phones at the age of 15 and above. The population above 15 would be the addressable population for mobile phones. As shown in the table below, this number would be about 28 million people.

Kenya 2016	
Total Population	48,000,000.00
Population above 15 years (58%)	27,840,000.00
Safaricom active base	25,100,000.00
Market share	90%

Table 11.1 Percentage of adult Kenyans carrying Safaricom lines

The 2016 Safaricom financial report gives the customer base as: '7.8% growth in customer base to 25.16m customers, *despite removing 1.7m customers from the count.*' They do not indicate why they have removed the 1.7 million customers.

So at the minimum, even ignoring the 1.7 million users that have been removed, this puts the number of people that have Safaricom lines at more than 90% of the addressable population. This is more in line with the revenue market share of about 88% in the market.

11.3 Informal nature of the Kenyan economy

What do Safaricom customers do with MPESA? Safaricom reports 7.3 chargeable transactions per active customer per month. A chargeable transaction as we have seen before is withdrawal transaction, a P2P transaction or a bill payment transaction. This population can also be divided neatly into two groups. There is a group who perform P2P and payment transactions and a group who withdraw cash.

Assuming for argument sake that the sending group and the withdrawing group are equal and exclusive, then the average numbers are more like,

- 14.8 send transactions and 0 withdrawal transaction for the sending group and
- 14.8 withdrawal transaction and 0 send transaction for the withdrawal group.

	2016
P2P transfers (Mn)	1,335
Withdrawals (Bn)	1,342
Other (Bn)	1,048
Total (Bn)	**3,725**
Active subs (Mn)	16.6
Transactions per sub	7.43
Total transactions (Mn)	1480.056
Average KES per transaction	2,516.80

Table 11.2 Average per P2P transaction value

This averages to a transaction every two days for each of the customers. Why are people sending money so often? Taking from the statistics again we see that the average chargeable transaction is KES 2,516 as per the table above.

These are not just 'send money home' transactions as claimed by most literature on the subject. Yes indeed send money home transactions make a very significant part of these transactions. However, more than half of these could actually be informal business transactions. These are customers paying for goods and service either remotely or over the counter directly to their supplier's personal accounts. It is worth noting that businesses operating informally do not separate the owner's money and money belonging to the businesses.

11.4 Social insurance and community development

In chapter 2 we saw that Kenya's insurance penetration is very low. This is because the society had for many years developed a system of community self-insurance. When a parent or relative or a neighbor is in hospital, the community contributes to pay the bills.

Distance does not hinder these contributions. People send money across the country to villages where they came from or where their parents, friends or relatives live as contributions for medical costs, funeral arrangement costs, wedding arrangements, and so on. As long as you have been contributing in your club, you know that when it is your day, the people will not desert you. This is some of the money we are seeing moving as P2P transactions.

Immediately after independence, the founding president came up with the concept of 'Harambee'. Harambee, literally meant pulling together. It largely involves pooling of resources. This was used for social developments a lot like crowd funding is used today for starting up economic entities. People pull together to raise funds to build schools, hospitals, churches and other similar community projects.

As in social insurance above, distance is no longer an object and it is not uncommon to get a text blast to members of a village living in the cities telling them that their former school now needs a new roof or some other similar project. Every person contributes and each amount, even one dollar equivalent is appreciated.

11.5 Mobile money is petty cash

Businesses usually keep what is known as petty cash for small transactions that do not need to go through the formal financial system but are instead processed together and booked as a batch. This is the same for individuals.

Take an individual with a bank account. They will probably pay school fees, rent/mortgage etc. through the bank. However, when they take their car for service, they pay the mechanic in cash or through mobile money. To fuel the car, it is most convenient for the service station to be paid through a highly liquid medium such as cash or mobile money.

This is of course significantly related to the item on informal business structure. An individual in the US will probably take their car to the dealership and make payment by cheque or through a card. The Texaco service station in the US dealership is probably owned by a large corporate entity. In Kenya it is owned by an individual. In fact, in rural towns the service stations are independent without any linkages to the major oil companies.

11.6 Other factors.

- National pride: The more M-PESA is lauded out there, the more powerful it grows in the country. Kenyans want the glory associated with the product and this keeps the growth momentum.
- Marketing: Safaricom is the biggest advertiser in the country and a significant amount of this advertising budget goes to M-PESA.

11.7 Proposed model

Once we agree that mobile money is good for the economy, the next question is how to implement it to ensure it succeeds in circumstances that are different from the ones that drove the Kenyan one.

Interoperability

As we saw earlier, the Kenyan system did not need interoperability because it was driven by the player with the highest market share (Safaricom). This in turn drove the player to be a monopoly.

The mobile money platforms in Kenya require the SIM card and HSM both of which have proprietary systems. These cannot be shared by operators. This then means that the system cannot be interoperable. However, Government has the ability to force the interoperability. There are various methods that the government can use to achieve this.

The most sensible one would be to force operators to share one platform. To do this, all the SIM cards sold in the country would have to have the same mobile money applet. The SMS originated from this app would then be sent to a central platform holder who should not be a telecoms operator. This would require a few accommodations. For example updates on the mobile money app would need to be done OTA (over the air) directly from the platform operator to each of the operator SIM.

Proposed ownership structure

The entity should be financed by government. However it should be shielded from government procurement and trade restrictions to enable growth and innovation. Once it stabilizes, the entity should then be offloaded to the telecoms, banks and agents as shown below strictly in the ratios of their activity. If a telecoms has been pushing it, they get more shares. Finally, once it becomes mature the government shareholding may then be offloaded to the public.

- 40% Central bank.
- 20% telecommunication entities
- 20% banking fraternity
- 20% agents

To a lot of academic and policy advisors, government involvement in private business is taboo. However, this is a project with a very significant impact in the wider economy and cannot be left to entities just looking at the profit motive. Furthermore mobile money could have a long payback horizon. It may not even break even in terms of profitability. However, from a macro-economic perspective, the economy would very significantly stand to benefit. Further

- The platform is expensive
- However, the project may not have immediate benefits. It took Safaricom 3 years to get a profit in the favorable circumstances it had in Kenya. It is likely to take longer in other economies. Government comes in to help midwife the process and take the initial risks.
- Government is able to force policy and processes in a particular direction. Here government will be able to nudge banks to co-operate and run in a particular direction.
- Mobile money can be very risky. See the case of MTN Uganda. Government is well equipped to absorb such risks.
- Whenever e-value is created in a mobile money ecosystem, the operator is issuing currency (albeit currency that is backed by cash). This should be managed very closely (at least in the early stages) by Central bank.
- While various telecommunication entities in various countries world over have tried interoperability, rates charged across entities are certainly going to be different. This cost differential will have the effect of discouraging transfers between networks and therefore depressing the overall use of mobile money. An even worse eventuality could be a situation where like the telecommunication situation in Kenya, customers could end up coalescing around one favorite entity either based on the on-net transfer cost or simply brand power with a resultant monopoly situation.
- Interoperability between mobile entities is a complex solution replicating bank interoperability involving clearing and settlement of

funds between and among the entities. Considering the revenues from the smaller entities, this could be a significantly expensive venture. The proposed model is such that all funds are held by one entity therefore do not require to be reconciled between the mobile entities.

Opposition
Obviously this model would have opposition from quite a number of quarters.

- Telecommunication entities who may already have invested in their own network.
- Banks who traditionally fight mobile money. This is because mobile money is an unknown quantity in the financial services sector and because it is digital could venture into every other sector that banks are in. In Kenya, banks have to accommodate M-PESA or risk losing customers.
- Analysts who believe that government should not get involved in business.

Other models
Other methods that could be investigated include:

- Get the system out of the SIM card.
- Run the system on USSD as do banks in Kenya. Problem is USSD can be complicated for most people.
- Run the platform on the web. Problem is internet may not be as widely available as 2G network.
- Adopt the Peruvian Model, BIM. This only started in 2016 so it is still too early to determine whether or not it will work.
- Indonesia interoperability model. This went live in mid-2013. However, Indonesia has not yet reported the stunning growth witnessed by M-PESA in 2008.
- Tanzania interoperability model sponsored by ifc.

References

Hassan et al, 2013: Retail payments and economic growth http://www.suomenpankki.fi/pdf/170343.pdf Retrieved 31 July 2016

Moody's Analytics 2016: The Impact of Electronic Payments on Economic Growth https://usa.visa.com/dam/VCOM/download/visa-everywhere/global-impact/impact-of-electronic-payments-on-economic-growth.pdf Retrieved 31 July 2016

Alliance for financial Inclusion: Enabling mobile money transfer The Central Bank of Kenya's treatment of M-PESA http://www.afi-global.org/sites/default/files/publications/afi_casestudy_mpesa_en.pdf Retrieved 31 July 2016

David Ndii: Financial landscape trends 2006 – 2009 http://fsdkenya.org/wp-content/uploads/2015/08/11-06-27_finaccess_09_results_analysis.pdf Retrieved 31 July 2016

THE KENYA POWER AND LIGHTING COMPANY LIMITED ANNUAL REPORT AND FINANCIAL STATEMENTS 2014/2015: http://kplc.co.ke/img/full/jSsYVq47rObE_KENYA%20POWER%20ANNUAL%20REPORT%202015%20-%20FOR%20WEB.pdf Retrieved 31 July 2016

Lachaal et al: Mobile Money Services, Regulation and Creating an Enabling Environment in Africa http://www.afdb.org/fileadmin/uploads/afdb/Documents/Publications/Economic_Brief_-_Mobile_Money_Services_Regulation_and_Creating_an_Enabling_Environment_in_Africa.pdf Retrieved 31 July 2016

Central Bank of Kenya: Bank Supervision and Banking Sector Reports https://www.centralbank.go.ke/index.php/bank-supervision-reports Retrieved 31 July 2016

Kenya Population (2016) Worldodometers Retrieved 31 July 2016

CBA now biggest retail bank with 10 million customers Business Daily 06 March 2015. Retrieved 31 July 2016

Insurance regulatory Authority: Insurance Industry Report For the year ended 31st December, 2014 http://www.ira.go.ke/attachments/article/134/Annual%20Report%202014%20%2012.10.2015%20Final.pdf Retrieved 31 July

The National Treasury: SPECIAL FEATURE: What you need to know about the M-Akiba bond: http://www.mygov.go.ke/?p=5052 Retrieved 31 July 2016

Retirement Benefits Authority: Mbao Pension Plan FAQs: http://www.rba.go.ke/index.php/en/component/content/article?id=56 Retrieved 31 July 2016

Western Union: Western Union Reports First Quarter Results http://s1.q4cdn.com/568883301/files/doc_news/Financial%20News/Earnings-Release-Q1-2016-FINAL-050316.pdf Retrieved 31 July 2016

Equity Group Holdings Limited: Financial Results: http://equitybankgroup.com/investor-relations/financial-results Retrieved 31 July 2016

Business Daily M-Kesho growth stalls over hitch on profit sharing.25 March 2012. Retrieved 31 July 2016

Michael Joseph looks back at M-PESA growth seven years later Business Daily 05 March 2014. Retrieved 31 July 2016

Kenya Commercial Bank: KCB Investors: https://www.kcbbankgroup.com/kcb-group-investors/ Retrieved 31 July 2016

Co-operative Bank: Investor Relations & Financial Results: https://www.co-opbank.co.ke/investor-relations-and-financial-results Retrieved 31 July 2016

SANS Institute InfoSec Reading Room: The GSM Standard (An overview of its security) https://www.sans.org/reading-room/whitepapers/telephone/gsm-standard-an-overview-security-317 Retrieved 31 July 2016

Financial Action Task Force: Risk-Based Approach Guidance for Money

Service Businesses http://www.fatf-gafi.org/media/fatf/documents/reports/Guidance-RBA-money-value-transfer-services.pdf Retrieved 31 July 2016

Neil Davidson and Paul Leishman: Building, Incentivising and Managing a Network of Mobile Money Agents: A Handbook for Mobile Network Operators http://www.gsma.com/mobilefordevelopment/wp-content/uploads/2011/02/Agent-Networks-full.pdf Retrieved 31 July 2016

Business Daily Chase Bank shocks market with Sh8bn secret insider loans 7 April 2016. Retrieved 31 July 2016

About the author

Stephen Muchiri has worked for more than twenty years in finance in various companies spread across diverse industries in Kenya. Twelve of those have been spent in the telecoms sector. He has spent times in integrated telecoms organizations, in mobile money and tower company entities at middle to senior levels. For any information regarding the mobile money industry in Kenya or general insights into the business, he can be reached at;

Email: skmuchiri2000@yahoo.com

LinkedIn: https://ke.linkedin.com/in/stephen-muchiri-96976622

www.ingramcontent.com/pod-product-compliance
Lightning Source LLC
Chambersburg PA
CBHW060348190526
45169CB00002B/527